PUSHKIN PRESS

THE MADMAN'S GUIDE TO STAMP COLLECTING

'Encyclopedic, curious, labyrinthine and surprising, like the work of Thomas De Quincey, Thomas Browne, Robert Burton'

Times Literary Supplement

'[A] delightful mishmash of quotations, digressions, obscure facts, arcane anecdotes and playful romps... *The Madman's Guide to Stamp Collecting* is a Cinderella book, though I am certain that the wonders it has to offer will not vanish on the stroke of midnight'

Literary Review

'I shed a tear at the end of this, Irwin's final work, recognising not just a fellow collector – of ideas, ephemera, stuff – but a fellow man emptying his pockets, as it were, at the end of a long life'

Spectator

ROBERT IRWIN (1946–2024) was a novelist, publisher, reviewer, Arabist and historian. He was a fellow of The Royal Society of Literature and the author of ten novels, including *The Arabian Nightmare*, *Satan Wants Me* and *Tom's Version*, as well as many works of non-fiction including *The Arabian Nights: A Companion* and *Memoirs of a Dervish*.

THE MADMAN'S GUIDE TO STAMP COLLECTING

-

Robert Irwin

PUSHKIN PRESS

Pushkin Press
Somerset House, Strand
London WC2R 1LA

First published by Pushkin Press in 2025
This edition published in 2026

ISBN 13: 978-1-80533-776-8

A CIP catalogue record for this title is available from the British Library

The authorised representative in the EEA is eucomply OÜ, Pärnu mnt. 139b-14, 11317, Tallinn, Estonia, hello@eucompliancepartner.com, +33757690241

Designed and typeset by Tetragon, London
Printed and bound in the United Kingdom by Clays Ltd, Elcograf S.p.A.

Pushkin Press is committed to a sustainable future for our business, our readers and our planet. This book is made from paper from forests that support responsible forestry.

MIX
Paper | Supporting responsible forestry
FSC® C018072
www.fsc.org

www.pushkinpress.com

1 3 5 7 9 8 6 4 2

THE MADMAN'S GUIDE TO STAMP COLLECTING

"THINGS SEEMED TO BE GOING QUITE WELL UNTIL A FEW MONTHS AGO WHEN I FOUND MYSELF BEING SUCKED INTO THE MURKY TWILIGHT WORLD OF PHILATELY..."

THE STAMP DEALER David Brandon is a recurrent figure in Simon Garfield's memoir, *The Error World*. 'There are lots of books about stamps,' he said, partly as a warning. 'And they don't really sell.'[1] This does not worry me as this is not that sort of book, for my book about stamp collecting will be of little or no practical use or interest to stamp collectors. It does not deal with the subject's practicalities. Instead, the following topics are covered: the Psychology and Psychopathology of Collecting; Seriality; Miniaturisation; Classification; Nostalgia; Anal Retentiveness; Specialisation; Fraudulence; Commemoration; Rarity; Completeness; Sexuality of Collecting; Secrecy and Subversion; Digressiveness; Boyhood; Dutchness; Boredom; Death. This book also gives madmen the opportunity to learn that they are not alone in their madness.

As a schoolboy I used to collect stamps. I specialised in stamps of the German states and Holland. Later, as a postgraduate student, I briefly collected stamps of Hejaz, Pahlavi Iran and Ottoman Turkey in order to get practice at reading Arabic and quasi-Arabic calligraphy. I don't collect stamps any more. I stopped in the 1970s. Until this book was all but complete I have refrained from looking at the stamp collection that I accumulated so many decades ago. My hope was that in its neglect it would have graduated into serving as a time capsule.

If I am no longer a stamp collector, why did I write this book? The truth is that its origin was uncanny. One night some forty years ago I dreamt that I arrived early at a party (as I so often do) and there across the room I saw my agent leaning against the mantelpiece and I went over to talk to him. 'Well, now that your last book has been so successful, we have to think what you should write next,' he said. 'Ah, I have it! Stamp collecting!' About two weeks later I arrived early at a real party and there, at the far side of the room, was my agent. I went over to him and told him my dream. He burst out laughing. Then he suddenly sobered up. 'Actually that is *not* such a bad idea.' Ever since then I have set aside a small notebook in which I have written down quotations and references to stamps and stamp collecting in unexpected places—so not in *Gibbons Stamp Monthly*, but in Ernst Gombrich's life of Aby Warburg and in Dennis Wheatley's *To the Devil a Daughter*. Then, when I set to writing this book, further intensive researches introduced me to authors I had previously known little or nothing about, including Samuel Beckett, Ellery Queen, Osip Mandelstam, Louise Erdrich and Ciaran Carson, as well as artists such as Kurt Schwitters, Joseph Cornell and Donald Evans. For me, just the discovery of the writings of the Belfast poet and fiction writer Ciaran Carson has made this project worthwhile.

As Walter Benjamin wrote in *One-Way Street*, 'Quotations in my work are like wayside robbers who leap out armed and relieve the stroller of his conviction.' *The Madman's Guide to Stamp Collecting* largely consists of quotations and in this respect it resembles Benjamin's *Arcades Project* and Roberto Calasso's

The Ruin of Kasch (and in Umberto Eco's *The Mysterious Flame of Queen Loana* there is a character who collects quotations on fog, and his book too will be discussed in what follows). The quotations argue with each other and, in so doing, they do most of my work for me. Since the labyrinthine and digressive nature of my book has been inspired (if that is indeed the right verb) by the writings of Thomas De Quincey, it seems appropriate to open with a quotation from him.

> Every moment are shouted aloud by the Post-Office servants the great ancestral names of cities known to history through a thousand years,—Lincoln, Winchester, Portsmouth, Gloucester, Oxford, Bristol, Manchester, York, Newcastle, Edinburgh, Perth, Glasgow—expressing the grandeur of the empire by the antiquity of its towns, and grandeur of the mail establishment by the diffusive radiation of its separate missions. Every moment you hear the thunder of lids locked down upon the mailbags. That sound to each individual mail is the signal for drawing off, which process is the finest part of the entire spectacle. Then come the horses into play;—horses! can these be horses that (unless powerfully reined in) would bound off with the action and gestures of leopards? What stir!—what sea-like ferment!—what a thundering of wheels, what a trampling of horses!—what farewell cheers—what redoubling peals of brotherly congratulation.[2]

Thomas De Quincey's account of his alleged night journey on a mail coach which sped through the night, carrying news of a great British victory at Talavera in 1809 against the French troops which Napoleon had sent into Spain, owed more to opium-fuelled visionary prose, nostalgia and literary self-display than it did to real memories. It is a stylish conjuring trick, writing produced 'on the brink of abysses'. The horn sounds, flags are flying and the horses, with their fiery eyeballs and dilated nostrils, are like creatures of the Apocalypse. The speed of the horses matches the fever in De Quincey's blood. Such speed is dangerous, and at times youthful exhilaration gives way to obsessive apprehension of danger and sudden death. 'Death the crowned phantom, with all the equipage of his terrors, and the tiger roar of his voice.' There is perhaps also a politico-religious subtext to this night journey, and a biographer of De Quincey has written of 'kaleidoscopic nightmares in which Napoleon's defeat at Waterloo is assimilated within a broader myth of Britain as a righteous colonial power charged by God with the task of preserving and extending Christian civilization'.[3]

The Post Office had established the mail-coach service in Britain in 1784. The service placed a ferocious emphasis on speed and hence the coaches would travel by night when there was much less traffic on the roads. They stopped only for the exchange of horses (at approximately every ten miles). The coachman would sound his post horn to give advance warning to the keepers of turnpike gates. It was against the law for the keepers or anyone else to get in the way of the speeding coach. The coach also took passengers, and young men like De Quincey paid extra for the excitement of sitting up front beside the coachman. A guard with a gun had a seat at the back of the coach. Yet, after all this racing through the countryside, there were frequent final delays in getting the post delivered, since it was not the sender who paid for delivery of the letter, and the recipient might be hard to find or reluctant to pay.

In *The English Mail-Coach* a haunted man looks back across forty years to the romance of those night-time races to deliver the mail. De Quincey's sublime masterpiece was first published in *Blackwood's Magazine* in 1849. (He would die in 1859.) Yet already by 1849 the spread of a network of railways across Britain from the 1830s onwards and the commencement of the penny post in 1840 had made De Quincey's high-flown, opium-soaked account of the excitements of these night journeys an evocation of an era that was all but over. The railways and the penny post changed everything and with that change the tranquil pursuit of philately became possible.

Mostly tranquil, anyway. But, as we shall see, the story of stamp collecting embraces murder, theft, strange erotic practices, conspiracy theories and various deep philosophies. This book is itself a *collection* of references to collecting and insights about that activity. The rarer and more improbable those references and insights are, the more pleased I am to have stumbled across them. In this literary collection, like so many other kinds of collection, rarity is something to be prized. To take just one example, in the nineteenth century, if a man wanted to check whether he was subject to nocturnal erections, then he might stick a row of perforated stamps round the base of his penis and, if in the morning he discovered that the row of stamps had torn at the perforations, then he would know that he had had a nocturnal erection. That is only the first of many useful revelations. (We shall return to the erotic aspects of stamp collecting later.) This anthology is a mosaic of fiction, philosophy, sociology, biography and autobiography. I repeat, I doubt it will be of much interest to real-life stamp collectors.

STAMP COLLECTING and its alleged boringness has had a poor press from quite a few writers and thinkers. William Inge (1860–1954), the Dean of St Paul's Cathedral and a prolific author and social commentator, was rechristened the 'gloomy dean' by the *Daily Mail* because of his hostility to the notions of progress and democracy, as well as his general misanthropy—and to all this we may add his contempt for philately. He was once asked, in what was presumably intended to be polite conversation, 'Are you interested in liturgy?' To which he replied, 'No. Neither do I collect postage stamps.' The Cambridge Regius Professor of History G.N. Clark's thinking ran along the same lines as Inge's. The medievalist Maurice Keen recalled an encounter with him.

'Long ago I once confessed to the historian G.N. Clark, my uncle by marriage, that I was interested in medieval chivalry. "Does that include heraldry?" he asked. "No," I said; "Good," said he; "I have always thought that for a historian heraldry stands about the same level as stamp collecting."'[4] When the physicist Ernest Rutherford (1871–1937) declared that 'All science is either physics or stamp collecting', it seems unlikely that he was being complimentary about the hobby. On the broader topic of hobbies, the writer and raconteur Quentin Crisp (1908–99) stated that 'Hobbies are instead of life. What is needed is a greater intensity of living style.' But 'life' might be overrated and, against Crisp, I can quote the American essayist Logan Pearsall Smith (1865–1946): 'People say life is the thing, but I prefer reading.' And there are surely some who prefer stamp collecting to life.

The novelist and essayist George Orwell (1903–1950) had mixed feelings about stamps and stamp collecting. In 1934 he worked in Booklovers' Corner, a second-hand bookshop in Hampstead, and he wrote a short article about his time there, 'Bookshop Memories' (published in *Fortnightly* in 1936). As a sideline to the book business, the shop had sold stamps to collectors. Orwell was obviously unenthusiastic about that clientele: 'stamp collectors are a strange, silent, fish-like breed, of all ages, but only of the male sex; women, apparently, fail to see the peculiar charm of gumming bits of coloured paper into albums'. And yet stamp collecting was an integral part of the Englishness that Orwell so loved. In his famous essay 'England Your England', he commented on an 'English characteristic which is so much a part of us that we barely notice it, and that is the addiction to hobbies and spare-time occupations, the *privateness* of English life. We are a nation of flower-lovers, but also a nation of stamp-collectors, pigeon-fanciers, amateur carpenters, coupon-snippers, darts-players, crossword-puzzle fans.' So the fish-like stamp collectors were as much part of his beloved country as the famous, though anonymous, 'old maids biking to Holy Communion through the mists of the autumn morning'. Orwell also conceded the educational value of stamp collecting. In a letter sent to Jack Common in 1939 he wrote that 'I suppose about 50 per cent of them know whereabouts Czechoslovakia was, but where is the Ukraine? And where are Memel and Eupen Malmedy, not to mention Russian Subcarpathia? The only people who can keep up these days are philatelists.'

Right from the beginning there was an idea that stamps might serve an educational purpose. Before he became an institutional innovator and a knighted public figure, Rowland Hill (1795–1879) had been a teacher. Headmaster of Hazelwood, an experimental school in Birmingham, he had spent twenty-five years as a teacher and educational reformer. He was an idealist who believed that the introduction of cheap postage would encourage working-class literacy. He introduced this strange thing, the postage stamp, in the following words, 'a bit of paper just large enough to bear the stamp and covered at the back with a glutinous wash which the bringer might by applying a little moisture, attach to the back of the letter'. Hill's proposed penny postal service, in which the sender rather than the recipient paid the postage, met with opposition from vested interests in Parliament. But during the first year of the Penny Black's introduction, 1840, the number of letters sent by mail more than doubled. (By the way, the Penny Black is not a rare stamp. How could it be? It was in use throughout Great Britain for decades and 68,808 were issued.) Hill had correctly calculated that a reduction in postal charges would result in an increase of use and therefore of revenue.

Apart from their role in encouraging literacy, there were of course various lessons to be learnt from the imagery carried by stamps—some of those lessons quite subtle. The future Marxist historian Eric Hobsbawm (1917–2012) was born in Alexandria in Egypt, the son of an official in Posts and Telegraphs. Subsequently the English-speaking family moved to Vienna where Hobsbawm went to school. He remembered how as a schoolboy in 1920s Austria he collected stamps:

> What children born in 1917 knew of the events of the still young twentieth century which were so alive in the minds of parents and grandparents—war, breakdown, revolution, inflation—was what adults told us or, more likely, what we overheard them talking about. The only direct evidence we had of them were the changing images on postage stamps. Stamp collecting in the 1920s, though it was far from self-explanatory, was a good introduction to the political history of Europe since 1914. For an expatriate British boy it dramatized the contrast between the unchanging continuity of George V's head on British stamps and the chaos of overprints, new names and new currencies elsewhere.[5]

In V.S. Naipaul's acclaimed novel *A Bend in the River* the bend in question has been successively 'a forest, a meeting place, an Arab settlement, a European outpost, a European suburb, a ruin like the ruin of a dead civilization, the glittering Domain of new Africa and now this'. The protagonist, Salim, a Muslim Indian, begins life on the coast of East Africa, but 'it came to me while I was quite young, still at school, that our way of life was antiquated and almost at an end'.

> Small things can start us off in new ways of thinking, and I was started off by the postage stamps of our area.
>
> The British administration gave us beautiful stamps. These stamps depicted local scenes and local things; there was one called 'Arab Dhow'. It was as though, in those stamps, a foreigner had said 'This is what is most striking about this place.' Without that stamp of the dhow I might have taken the dhows for granted. As it was, I learned to look at them. Whenever I saw them tied up at the waterfront I thought of them as something peculiar to our region, quaint, something the foreigner would certainly remark on, something not quite modern, and certainly nothing like the liners and cargo ships that berthed in their own modern docks.[6]

And 'it was Europe that gave us the descriptive postage stamps that gave us our ideas about what was picturesque about ourselves' (p.268).

Such thoughts led Salim to try look at things from a distance.

Increasingly his sense that his people had fallen behind heightens his sense of personal insecurity. There is no redemption from the past, only gathering darkness. So he migrates from East Africa to set up a general store in what is evidently the Congo (subsequently renamed Zaire) and Naipaul's novel becomes a meditation on the dismal ruination of the Congo and the alienation of its inhabitants.

Salim definitely had a point. To take a real-life example, as long as Egypt was a formal British protectorate and, after 1922, an unofficial one until the 1950s, the images on its stamps dwelt overwhelmingly on Egypt's ancient and picturesque past which was Pharaonic: the Pyramids, a Nile felucca, the Temple of Abu Simbel, the statue of Cleopatra at Dendera—oh, and a little British dam at Aswan. The Islamic history of Egypt—the Arab conquests, the Abbasids, Fatimids, Mamluks and Ottomans—was obliterated in this antiquarian bias. The only significant exceptions were the portraits of the Khedive Fuad I and, after his death in 1922, his successor Farouq. (Incidentally Farouq was a noteworthy collector. He collected Fabergé eggs, aspirins, old coins, razor blades, Geiger counters and stamps. His stamp collection, which was one of the most valuable in the world, was sold by auction two years after he was deposed in 1952.) It was only once the Khedival rule and informal British protectorate came to an end and a Nasserist republic was established in 1953 that one finds stamps featuring images of the Cairo Electronics Exhibition, Egypt's youth, an agricultural labourer, the defence of Port Said and so forth.

TESTIMONIALS to the educational value of stamp collecting are found in unexpected places. In the poet Louis Aragon's Surrealist novel, *Le Paysan de Paris* (1926; *The Paris Peasant*) I found the following:

> O philately, philately: you are a most strange goddess, a slightly foolish fairy, and it is you who take by the hand the child emerging from the enchanted forest in which little Tom Thumb, the Blue Bird, Little Red Riding Hood and the Wolf have finally gone to sleep side by side; it is you, too, who illustrate Jules Verne and who transport over the oceans on brightly coloured paper wings those hearts least prepared for the voyage. Those who, like me, got their first idea of the Sudan from a small carmine-bordered rectangle in which a white burnous mounted on a mahari advances on a sepia background, those who were familiar with the Emperor of Brazil imprisoned within his oval frame, with the giraffes of Nyasaland and the Australian swans, with Christopher Columbus discovering America in violet, will understand what I mean! But the tiresome reflections which adorn the window display we are in the process of contemplating no longer belong to those multi-valued series we used

> to know. Edward VII looks like a monarch from ancient times. Great adventures have shaken those childhood companions of ours, the stamps which a thousand bonds of mystery unite with world history. Here are the newcomers which take into account a recent and incomprehensible reshuffling of global boundaries. Here are the stamps of defeats, the stamps of revolutions.[7]

Note Aragon's nostalgia first for his passage out of infancy, which the dignified imagery of stamps assisted, and then his increasing unease about the evidence of global insecurity that had been signalled by the more recent stamps. It will be necessary to return to *Le Paysan de Paris*.

The passage out of infancy must lead with a horrid inevitability to consideration of the topic of Freudianism. In 'Character and Anal Eroticism' (1908) Sigmund Freud (1856–1939) had stressed the significance of early problems in toilet training, specifically regarding defecation, for the development of character later in life. The infant has resented the loss of control over his bowels. Freud described the anal-retentive type of adult as being preoccupied with orderliness, parsimony and obstinacy. Later Freud and his followers would go on to identify a propensity for forming collections as a further characteristic of the anal-retentive type. The collector seeks an object of desire. Surprisingly the crucial prototype object of desire is shit. Freud thought that the collector is a person who, without knowing it, is seeking to recover the faeces lost due to the lack of bowel control in the infant years. It is this unconscious drive that will form the anally retentive personality of an adult who will seek to create a collection of something or other that he can control, organise and rearrange. Interestingly Freud himself was famous as a collector, having acquired a collection of some 2,500 antiquities which he kept in his study, with some favoured pieces on his writing desk. In addition to antiquities he also collected Chinese and Greek vases, exemplary psychoanalytic cases, jokes, Jewish anecdotes, dreams and errors. Did Freud diagnose himself as having an anally retentive personality? Marshall, the protagonist of *The Stamp Collector*, the novel by David Benedictus (1938–2023), was not impressed by this sort of thing: 'Then there was a supercilious article he had once read, not in a stamp magazine, but in a superior Sunday supplement, about collectors. It said that stamp collectors were anally obsessed, repressed homosexuals . . . (Marshall was not sure what the anus had to do with it.)'[8]

According to John Forrester, a prolific writer on Freud and Freudianism, 'Following Susan Stewart's fine analysis in her book *On Longing* (1984), we can see that Freud's objects (the antiques and texts) served both the functions of evoking the past, of entering into the nostalgic dimension of the souvenir, and of effacing the past, of building a new timeless world of the collection.' A child's learning to control, that is to possess the contents of his bowels, gives him or her an early sense of being in control of something. Later in adult life possessiveness always betrayed anxiety. 'I can't live without it!' Freud thought of himself as a conquistador who would explore and conquer the new world of psychoanalysis.[9] Since Freud had invented this new world, it was perhaps easy for him to conquer it. Other psychoanalytically minded theorists have suggested that the male penchant for collecting might be a substitute for erotic conquests.

Donald Winnicott (1896–1971) was a British psychiatrist and psychoanalyst, much of whose research was centred on child analysis. In his findings he placed great stress on transitional objects in childhood, such as teddy bears. Playing with such objects made a sort of path all the way up to such eventual adult pursuits as business and politics. His theory of object relations was set out in a paper entitled 'Transitional Objects and Transitional Phenomena', which was published in the *International Journal of Psychoanalysis*, 34 (1953). Winnicott presented the transitional object as something which protected the infant from loneliness. His ideas about transitional objects in infancy were further developed by Werner Muensterberger (1913–2011). Muensterberger was an American citizen of German origin who became a famous psychoanalyst, and who was also well known for his collection of African art. Muensterberger, who acknowledged an intellectual debt to Winnicott, presented collecting as a way, commonly an irrational way, to soothe traumas or anxieties that had their origins in childhood and in particular the separation from one's mother. (As it happened, Muensterberger's mother died when he was still a boy, and at around the same time he started collecting African art.) In 1994 he published *Collecting: An Unruly Passion*, an influential and rather repetitive series of essays which took a psychoanalytic approach to the subject.[10] Having defined collecting as 'the selective gathering, and keeping of objects of subjective value', he took an oddly patronising view of the activity. Collectors were portrayed as damaged personalities who have been driven to collect in attempts to repair traumas experienced in early infancy. Collecting 'echoes emotions that have their roots in old affective experiences of oneness; in early sensations of wish fulfilment, and in relief of the child's anxiety and frustration that comes with feeling helpless and alone. Objects in the collector's experience, real or imagined, allow for a magical escape into a remote and private world . . . Since it represents an experience of triumph in defence against anxiety and the fear of loss, the return must be effected over and again . . . Not surprisingly, these phenomena have their root in early childhood. They originate in the baby's experiences not simply with hunger and satiety but with the subjective perception of closeness and belief, or, negatively, doubt in magical control' (pp.15–16). Again: 'What is prevalent is a need for reassertion in order to undo an old narcissistic wound. The objects are meant to give a sense of affirmation and magical support' (p.43). Also: 'Irrespective of individual idiosyncrasies of collectors, and no matter what or how they collect, one issue is paramount: the objects in their possession are all ultimate, often unconscious assurances against despair and loneliness' (p.48).

And again: 'When a better or more desirable object is found in someone else's possession by a collector, complicated emotions arise—admiration, envy, a notion of anxiety, distress, feelings of inferiority, in extreme cases, rage—no one of which excludes any of the others. There is a logic to such various responses:

insofar as these objects are magic-laden they imply that the owner is endowed with greater power than you. This leads to a feeling of potential subjugation and subsequently to a need for reaffirmation by the way of symbolic equivalents. And because of their unconscious link with the instinct for self-preservation, such needs must not be frustrated' (pp.141–2). And one more: '"collectibles" are, strictly speaking, implements that are meant to enhance or restore a narcissistically injured person's self' (p.235). So it is very clear that we are to understand that collectors of anything are among the world's walking wounded. They are inadequate, delusional, narcissistic fantasists. At best, Muensterberger's evidence for this is anecdotal, but mostly his thesis is based on sheer repetitive assertion and a great deal of it reads like autobiographical self-analysis posing as science.

The longest chapter in the book is devoted to Honoré de Balzac's novel *Le Cousin Pons* (1847) and the hypothetical common identity of Balzac and his creation Pons as collectors. Yet it is doubtful whether Balzac was a collector in the same sense that millions of ordinary collectors of, say, postage stamps, or cigarette cards or Ming porcelain are. True, Balzac was an extravagant accumulator of furnishings, paintings, tableware and what-not. So *Le Cousin Pons* has been read by Muensterberger as a kind of self-portrait of the author as collector. But was Balzac really a collector? And how much did Pons have in common with Balzac? To return to Muensterberger's definition of collecting as 'the selective gathering, and keeping of objects of subjective value', Balzac did accumulate objects, but not in any selective or specialised way. He did not become particularly knowledgeable about what he had acquired, nor did he take care to hang on to what he had purchased. Instead he bought furniture, dishes, plates, hangings and other stuff in order to impress his guests. It was as if he had set out to furnish a series of stage sets in which his literary success could be celebrated and admired. If he ran out of cash, and he often did, then the furnishings and paintings were sold without compunction.

Was Pons a self-portrait of Balzac? First, the story, which is primarily about a contested inheritance rather than collecting, was based on a short story by Albéric Second, a friend of Balzac's. Secondly, Balzac shows Pons to be a collector with an obsessive passion for visual beauty, and one who was intensely knowledgeable about what he had acquired. He lives for art and eating (and it is true that Pons and Balzac shared a passion for food). As Pons falls mortally ill, philistine parasites plot to loot what he had acquired. *Le Cousin Pons* is one of several Balzac novels that are primarily about contested legacies.

The Italian expert on decadent literature and on interior decoration, Mario Praz (1896–1982), is another of Muensterberger's case studies (or should that be victims?) in *Collecting*. *The Romantic Agony*, a study of Romantic eroticism and cruel fantasies in the late eighteenth and nineteenth century, is one of Praz's best-known books. *The House of Life* is quite different. First published in Italian as *La casa della vita* in 1958, it is a coolly erudite tour of a magnificent flat in Rome that he inhabited for several decades.[11] He papered and furnished the flat with things he had collected from the Empire and Regency periods. As he takes the reader from room to room, Praz shows off their arrangement, discourses on their materials and styles of decoration and reminisces about how he came to acquire some of his treasures. 'There is a secret magnetic force which attracts things to the man who desires them' (p.265). It was for him simultaneously a journey into a Napoleonic past and an exploration of his own memories.

He had managed to create a fairy tale in which he could live and in which 'there is a feeling of tension in the stillness, and sometimes the ear seems to catch the sound of faint stirrings, imperceptibly smothered, muffled, as in Stravinsky's *Firebird*. The house is a wood like the wood of the Sleeping Beauty; as in a great room, brightly lit and deserted, whose doors will soon be thrown open for a ball, as in a church, solemn, glowing with light, where soon, to the sound of an organ, a procession will advance from the sacristy, so a sense of expectation, of mingled anxiety and jubilation, quivers in the air of this house which, as all its visitors admit, even if in certain ways it seems like a museum, is yet a living museum, not a lifeless assemblage of objects' (p.327). And at the end of it all, he confesses that 'in the course of the years, I see myself as having myself become an object and an image, a museum piece among museum pieces, already detached and remote, and . . . I have looked at myself in a convex mirror, and I have seen myself no bigger than a handful of dust' (p.550).

Muensterberger, who met Praz sometime in the 1960s, found him to be 'a small, unimpressive man' who had written that his interests tended to turn into manias. As Praz put it: 'the mania for Empire furniture, the mania for books of emblems, the mania for Russian, just as, when a child, I had the mania for dolls and statuettes of saints and, as a boy, a mania for stamps' (pp.25–6). The boyhood passion for stamps is confirmed in *The House of Life* when he looked back on an occasion when he wanted to go to a particular library in Rome: 'not for books but for stamps, for they sold collectors' stamps there also and on the previous evening I had been eyeing a series of showy stamps, from Borneo possibly, which I was longing to secure for myself now that my mother had given me the money to buy them' (p.189). But we learn no more about the stamps, since he goes on to give an account of how the visit to the library was unwillingly forestalled by an outing to a place called Antella which was his first proper introduction to Italian rural life. Still it seems safe to guess that the boyhood mania for collecting stamps served as an apprenticeship for the grown man's collection of furniture, waxes, busts, prints, paintings, embroidery and other relics of a past century.

According to Muensterberger, 'Praz spoke of the beginnings of his collection but persistently stressed the considerable links with his unhappy personal life', which included a short-lived marriage. Muensterberger judged that Praz's passion for accumulated objects betokened 'an almost erotic excitement'. A club foot contributed to his loneliness and sense of inadequacy, particularly during the years of the First World War. In the long run his collecting Empire furniture and decorative objects 'had become a primary means for sublimating if not healing the trauma of his physical infirmity and an over-compensation for seeing himself as an outcast'.[12] A sad man indeed if we must take Muensterberger's word for all this. Yet if *Collecting* had been written with a fraction of the eloquence, erudition, self-awareness and fond evocations of earlier years that distinguishes the masterpiece that is *The House of Life*, then one might more easily be persuaded by Muensterberger's contentions. As for the man he sought to patronise, the distinguished American literary critic Edmund Wilson wrote in 'The Genie of the Via Giulia' that Praz 'will come to be known to posterity—so far as a foreigner can judge—as one of the best Italian writers of his time'.

Muensterberger was not a hard-line Freudian and he wrote that 'I am not in accord with certain psychoanalytic propositions according to which "cupidity and collecting mania . . . have their correlating determinants in the infantile attitude toward feces." This, I believe, is too confining a point of view. It is a homogenization on the basis of appearances and genetic phases instead of seeing the phenomenon in its immediate experiential context' (p.229). Here he was specifically criticising a proposition by Otto Fenichel in *The Psychoanalytic Theory of Neurosis*,[13] Yet Muensterberger was still possessed by the notion that collecting was necessarily the sign of an inward lack or deformity.

The Russian-born writer Ayn Rand (1905–82), author of the right-wing libertarian novels *The Fountainhead* (1943) and *Atlas Shrugged* (1957), presented, what seems to me, a positive and much more convincing portrait of collecting based on her own experience of this activity. This took the form of a short article,

'Why I Like Stamp Collecting', which was published in *Minkus Stamp Journal* in 1971. As a girl in Russia, Rand had collected stamps between the ages of ten and twelve before giving it up, but more than fifty years later she returned to the hobby:

> Only now the feeling had the eagerness of childhood combined with the full awareness, freedom and confidence of age . . . The pleasure lies in a certain way of using one's mind. Stamp collecting is a hobby for busy, purposeful, ambitious people . . . because, in pattern, it has the essential elements of a career, but transposed to a clearly delimited, intensely private world.[14]

She argued that creating a stamp collection involved decisions, choices and advances towards a goal and this made it a long-range activity. Of course collecting met the hard-working person's need for a change of track in order to relax, but essentially stamp collecting involved the same mental activity as planning and making a career. But, unlike the career, problem solving was not involved. The stamp collector entered a 'brotherhood' of the like-minded. 'It is a world for orderly, rational minds.' She asked herself, why specifically stamps? She answered: 'Because stamps are the concrete, visible symbols of an enormous abstraction: of the communications net embracing the world.' The postal system was a great global achievement (as John Updike similarly had argued, and we will get to him). Rand is perhaps one example among many of an adult who resumes stamp collecting and, in doing so, seeks to return to his or her childhood but with adult powers. Towards the end of her article Rand commended Iceland, Japan and Ryukyu as leaders in beautiful designs.

TO RETURN BRIEFLY to Freud, as his collection of figurines suggests, he was fascinated by antiquity. He believed that psychoanalysis was a form of archaeology. His final publication, *Moses and Monotheism* (1939), was an exercise in ancient history in which he sought to prove that Moses, the founder of monotheism, was actually an Egyptian. Many have regarded this exercise as an ingenious fantasy. The German cultural historian Aby Warburg (1866–1929) had no time for Freud and took quite a different view of antiquity. He belonged to a wealthy banking family and consequently was able to pursue a career as a private scholar in Hamburg and to build up a considerable personal library. (He collected stamps as well as books and photographs.) His younger brother took over the bank in exchange for funding Aby's book purchases. That was a substantial financial commitment, for by 1911 the older brother had acquired a private library of nearly 15,000 books.[15] The famous art historian Kenneth Clark described the life-changing impact on him by his attendance at a lecture given by Warburg in Rome in 1927:

> Warburg was without doubt the most original thinker on art history of our time, and entirely changed the course of art-historical studies. His point of view could be described as a reaction against the formalistic or stylistic approach of Morelli or Berenson. But I am sure that this was not his intention, because from the first his mind moved in an entirely different way. Instead of thinking of works of art as life-enhancing representations he thought of them as symbols, and he believed that the art historian should concern himself with the origin, meaning and transmission of symbolic images. The Renaissance was his chosen field, partly because Renaissance art contained a large number of such images . . . Symbols are a dangerous branch of study as they easily lead to magic; and magic leads to loss of reason.[16]

(Warburg had suffered a mental breakdown in 1918. In 1920 he had had to be hospitalised and it took him years to recover.)

One of the strange tasks Aby Warburg had set himself was to trace the afterlife of ancient Greek and Roman iconography in, among other things, the postage stamps of his own time. He specialised in the *Nachleben*, the afterlife of classical Antiquity and the survival of its imagery into modern times. This kind of iconographic activity amounted to a Romantic resurrection which Warburg described as 'ghost stories for adults'. Renaissance painters and subsequently Rembrandt and others had studied the ancient sarcophagi and triumphal arches and learned from the gestures of the carved figures on them how passion and movement should be depicted. Gestures encoded ideas. Warburg particularly interested himself in the *Pathosformel*, the term he used to designate the language of passionate gesture. Life and movement could be suggested by the play of wind on a woman's hair or dress. But the real interest of the afterlife of such gestures lay in the *Distanz* (distance) between the original intention of the imagery on, say, sarcophagi and the new meanings that Renaissance and later artists gave to those same gestures. For example, 'the ecstatic nymph' in Greek sculpture and painting, identifiable by floating and flying drapery, was in its earliest appearances best understood as embodying a kind of Dionysian passion, but from the eighteenth century onwards was oddly interpreted by art historians as an image of Apollonian order. Moreover, in time the devices that high art had stolen from antique mausoleums and victory arches would be borrowed and adapted for lesser media and new materials such as postage stamps. The fifteenth-century portrayal of a woman bearing fruit in Ghirlandaio's *Birth of St John the Baptist* in the Tornabuoni Chapel in Florence, which derived from the ancient image of the *nympha*, became in turn the ancestress of 'La Semeuse' (The Sower), a female figure who with minor variations featured on the standard range of French postage stamps from 1903 to 1938.

Warburg's library was organised in four broad categories: 'orientation', 'images', 'ideas' and 'action'. Warburg was keen that the more detailed library classifications should cut across traditional specialisms and he hoped that a scholar's quest for a certain book might lead to surprising and even more desirable finds among the books which were neighbours to the book that was initially being sought. 'The essential thing is to obey what Aby Warburg called the "law of the good neighbour",' according to Roberto Calasso (on whom more below), as Calasso described how his own library was organised: 'When looking for a book, you may discover that you were in fact looking for the book next to it.'[17]

A devoted group of brilliant scholars, many of them experts in iconography, gathered round Warburg and made use of his library. When Warburg had his mental collapse, the library was turned into an institute and, when the Nazis came to power in 1933, the library and the scholars who made use of it moved to Bloomsbury in London. Eventually the Warburg Institute and its library became part of the University of London. Inspection of the shelves of the library can be a weird education in itself, as one finds oneself contemplating books and articles on such arcane subjects as earth eating or the prehistory of aviation. After the philosopher and historian of ideas Ernst Cassirer was shown round the library, he remarked: 'This library is dangerous. I shall either have to avoid it altogether or imprison myself here for years.' The library also holds a surprising number of stamp catalogues and related books on philately.

According to the historian Simon Schama, Warburg believed that tracking a 'motif from archaic sources through all the mutations and permutations of form and meaning over time would not only yield deep connections between past and present; it would also reveal somewhere along that road, its cultural and cognitive significance for human apprehension. This was not just art history, not even cultural history. It was the pursuit of truth, revealed not in some vast metaphysical Platonic design, but as a part-coloured mosaic of discrete pieces of our nature from which a coherent image might emerge. It was, in fact, like a stamp album. Warburg loved postage stamps and was a passionate collector. And since he believed that nothing was too picayune to carry the imprint of an ancient motif, he was as likely to lecture on stamps (as well as heraldry, signs of the zodiac, pageants) as on the repository of his great stock of memory.'[18]

Warburg was at least as interested in the imagery of popular and ephemeral art forms as he was in the great artistic masterpieces. 'This included the design of postage stamps and in the summer of 1927, he arranged an exhibition of postage stamps, offering a typology of their imagery, portraits, landscapes, heraldry, but concentrating in particular on the fate of classical symbolism.'[19] He remained a stamp collector for most of his life and had a special interest in airmail stamps. After the Pact of Locarno was signed in 1925 and its three signatories were awarded the Nobel Prize in the following year, Warburg 'had an airmail stamp designed which showed a plane thrusting upward and bearing the inscription "Idea Vincit." The aircraft was to symbolise the victorious idea of Europe which Warburg hoped would emerge as a new reality from the horrors of the Great War in a new era of peace.'[20] He was also very interested in zeppelins. He had been enormously impressed by Hugo Eckener's captaincy of the first crossing of the Atlantic in the Graf Zeppelin in 1928 since he seemed to see this as a presage of Man's conquest of the cosmos.

According to Schama, 'his last project, which was called Mnemosyne, was in effect a gigantic vertical stamp album'. Warburg did not regard his collection of images as ephemera, but rather as 'evidence of longevity, of endurance, of an inescapable haunting'.[21] The aim was to assemble collections of related images—reproductions of artworks, postcards, newspaper clippings, advertisements, postage stamps and other ephemera— on a series of large panels. For example, Panel 77 includes reproductions of Eugène Delacroix's *Furious Medea* and *Scenes of the Massacre at Chios*; a ten-drachma coin of ancient Syracuse featuring Arethusa; two images from golf competitions; fish recipes; the French stamp of 'La Semeuse'; the Great Seal of Britain portraying Charles II as Neptune; and two stamps from Barbados, which feature Queen Victoria on a chariot of seashells. When Charles was portrayed in the likeness of Neptune as described in the *Aeneid*, one should not understand that the aim was to assert the identity of the two figures, but should recognise 'a dynamic symbol with metaphoric distance achieved through archaeologizing mnemic catharsis'.[22] (Mnemosyne, by the way, was the goddess of memory and mother of the Muses. A mneme is a person's capacity for retaining the after-effects of a particular experience or stimulation.)

Warburg's study of artistic and popular imagery was driven by his fascination with the idea of a social mneme. But more specifically the zoologist and evolutionary biologist Richard Semon (1859–1918) had postulated the existence of an organic collective memory which was based on the inheritance of acquired characteristics. People's nerves were altered by what they had experienced and in this fashion what they had experienced was passed on to the next generation. So Semon believed that this variant of Lamarckianism, or inheritance of acquired attributes, applied to social developments over the centuries. A mnemic trace or engram would be revived when a similar experience was encountered in a later generation. Thus heredity became a form of memory. Semon's concept of the engram, a permanent impression made by a stimulus or experience, is somewhat similar to Thomas De Quincey's notion of the involute (and we must come to that later). Semon's ideas were briefly fashionable, though they were soon discredited after his death. But Warburg obstinately continued to reflect on Semon's ideas and for Warburg his library and the Mnemosyne project were materialisations of his memory.

The Mnemosyne project was not regarded by Warburg as a finished demonstration of a fixed body of knowledge; it was instead a *Denkinstrument* (a tool to think with) whose unexpected juxtapositions might lead to new ideas and further juxtapositions. It was not finished and probably never could have been finished. Some of his colleagues seem to have thought that Warburg's tendency to free-associate about miscellaneous images hinted at a streak of residual madness. In its limitless and unachievable ambition the *Bilderatlas* (atlas of images) that was to be the concrete outcome of the Mnemosyne project can be compared to Benjamin's *Arcades Project*, and we shall also come to that great work eventually.

NOT ALL IMAGES were benign and in the 1920s Warburg came to believe that the fasces of Fascist Italy embodied a menacing reality. On the other hand, he worried about the emotional health of an imageless democracy and how that could be understood. He was perhaps right to do so. Modern artists and iconographers are mostly less familiar with classical heritage than their predecessors used to be. In the nineteenth and early twentieth centuries stamps were more often than not designed by artists who were familiar with the imagery of Antiquity and the Italian Renaissance. The imagery of their stamps made reference to ancient *Romanitas*—wreaths, columns, fasces and lightly tripping nymphs.

But the rot started with the issuing of commemorative stamps, though Britain bravely resisted this unwelcome trend until 1924 when, with George V's reluctant agreement, commemorative stamps were issued to mark the opening of the British Empire Exhibition. More broadly other countries were already issuing sets of stamps which were not primarily designed to be used for postage and instead were mostly produced to be sold to collectors. Had Warburg lived on into the twenty-first century he would have found it pretty difficult to trace the *Nachleben* of

Antiquity in gaudy sets of stamps devoted to Cinderella, rocket science and recently deceased popstars. In the past there has been quite a lot of criticism by philatelists of the General Post Office and the vulgarity of the catchpenny commemoratives designed to attract collectors. It was something which came in with Tony Benn when he became Postmaster General in 1964. He tried but failed to remove the queen's head from British stamps. Up until the mid-1930s the Post Office believed that the stamp was a symbol of a contract between the purchaser and the Crown and hence the inclusion of the monarch's head in all designs. In his study of the semiotics of stamp design David Scott had this to say:

> Icons should always have a real link with the indexical function of the stamp which supports them; they should not, as in some recent colonial designs, merely offer images of Second World War aircraft, vintage cars, or *The Magic Roundabout*, labels which are not stamps in the true sense of the word but mere 'icons', stickers for the collections of juveniles.[23]

For a philatelic purist like Simon Garfield, the 1860s was the heyday of British stamp design.

The vulgarisation of stamp imagery was also roundly denounced in Benedictus's *The Stamp Collector*. Having suggested that older stamps were beautiful because of their honesty, the author continued:

> Latterly stamps were produced by greedy countries with the requirements of dealers in the forefronts of their minds. The simple process of planting a letter was no longer paramount. Greed and self-consciousness had taken over from naïf artistry. Who really wanted to stick vulgar reproductions of Rubenesque nudes on their envelopes? Things became so decadent that some countries seemed to have no raison d'être other than to issue stamps. The Tongans issued weirdly shaped stamps like jigsaw pieces, or blatantly coloured ones like luggage labels, or circular ones like gold coins.

Ayn Rand had a similar complaint: 'some countries are putting out an unconscionable amount of philatelic waste, more than could possibly be used for normal philatelic needs'. Benedictus laments what has been lost: 'But in the first issues, patriotism, dignified symbolism, a flair for colour and a delight in the crafts of engraving and printing combined to produce not just beauty, but rare beauty.'[24] The varied colours of the first issues of Nova Scotia were cited by Benedictus as exemplars.

The novelist and fiction writer Francis Spufford (b.1964) has further drawn attention to the spurious connections between many stamp issues and the territories of their supposed issue:

> Signs and symbols of authority (like a flag, like a pistol volley) which referred to organisations of *people*, were carried where they no longer referred to anything. These days anyone can participate in the same fiction by collecting the postage stamps

issued for the different national zones of the Antarctic. Printed in Europe or Latin America or Australasia, never used except by scientists and soldiers posted (in a realer sense) to Antarctic bases, the coloured commemorative sets still look nice in albums. They are the trimmings of a sovereignty that only exists in trimmings.[25]

NOW AT LAST to return to Warburg, he used to correspond with another famous stamp collector, Walter Benjamin, though neither Warburg nor Benjamin was actually famous for being a stamp collector. Walter Benjamin (1892–1940), a German Jewish writer, is famous as a Marxist cultural theorist and essayist. He grew up in Berlin and studied at its university and at Munich and Bern. He published early essays on Baudelaire and did research on the origins of Baroque German drama, but thereafter he failed to follow an academic career. His interest in Marxism was strangely intertwined with an obsessive fascination with Jewish mysticism (and later Surrealism would provide a third thread). His deep interest in Jewish mysticism led to a life-long friendship and extensive correspondence with Gershom Scholem (1897–1982), the great scholar of Cabalism, Hassidism and other forms of

Jewish mysticism. Benjamin collected books (specialising in children's books and books written by mad people), as well as toys and stamps. Scholem was to write of his friend that while many of his books were for use, they were also contemplative objects that served as stimuli for reverie. He said that his library evokes 'memories of cities in which I found so many things'.

The American cultural critic Susan Sontag (1933–2004) phrased this more strongly: 'Book-hunting, like the sexual hunt, adds to the geography of pleasure—another reason for strolling about in the world. In collecting, Benjamin experienced what in himself was clever, successful, shrewd, unabashedly passionate.'[26] At this point it is time to digress and leave the account of Benjamin's collections (before I had really started) and consider what Sontag, a leading commentator on the works of Benjamin, had to say about collecting in general. Sontag had studied philosophy in Harvard, Oxford and Paris. Thereafter she lectured in New York and turned to creative writing, though the first of her writings to attract a lot of attention was her collection of non-fiction essays, *Against Interpretation* (1964). She went on to produce interpretative essays on difficult writers like Artaud, Barthes, Godard—and Benjamin.

The best-selling *The Volcano Lover* (1991), her most successful novel, deals with the lives of Sir William and Emma Hamilton in the Kingdom of Naples and the disruption to their lives in the 1790s brought about by the French invasion of Italy, the arrival of Admiral Horatio Nelson in Naples and the notorious affair between Horatio and the foul-mouthed but voluptuous Emma

Hamilton. Her husband, William, is the 'volcano lover', the adoring student of Vesuvius. He is not only an obsessive collector of lava specimens but also of Renaissance and Mannerist paintings, books, manuscripts and antiquities. Among other things, Sontag's novel serves as a vehicle for a series of meditations drawn from her long-standing preoccupation with the nature of collecting and collectors. To make some of her points she occasionally steps outside the fictional framework and abandons narrative fiction altogether in order to produce mini-essays on events and developments in the nineteenth and twentieth centuries. Indeed the novel opens with a very brief prelude in which the author finds herself hesitating outside a flea market. In real life Sontag collected books, pebbles and seashells. Later in *The Volcano Lover* there are interesting digressions on such matters as the destruction by a madman of the British Museum's Portland Vase in 1845, the origins of Puccini's opera *Tosca* (premiered in 1900) and the doomed fate of William Beckford's Fonthill Abbey, whose tower collapsed for the third and final time in 1825. The fabulously wealthy Beckford (1759–1844), the author of that marvellous Gothic fantasy novel *Vathek*, featured in *The Volcano Lover*, as he was a distant relative of William Hamilton and, like him, a notable collector, in Beckford's case of books, oriental objects, ceramics, statues and French furniture. Beckford outlived Hamilton, his wife and Nelson by several decades.

As the novelist John Banville put it in a review of *The Volcano Lover* in the *New York Times*: 'Throughout her novel the author will return repeatedly to the dichotomies of love and money, art and value, possession and renunciation.'[27] Sir William, in a curiously distancing fashion, is almost never referred to by that name and he is instead identified as the 'Cavaliere', just as Emma is normally referred to as 'his wife' and Horatio Nelson is always (mockingly?) 'the hero'. At times I felt as though I was not reading a novel, but rather Sontag's report on a novel. The Cavaliere is the collector par excellence. He likes to admire things and he collects in order to stave off melancholy:

> As a child he collected coins, then automata, then musical instruments. Collecting expresses a free-floating desire that attaches itself and re-attaches itself—it is a succession of desires. The true collector is in the grip not of what is collected but of collecting. By his early twenties the Cavaliere had already formed and been forced to sell, in order to pay debts, several small collections of paintings . . . To collect is to rescue things, valuable things, from neglect, from oblivion, or simply from the ignoble destiny of being in someone else's collection rather than one's own.[28] [Note Sontag's lapidary paratactic style.]

Sontag associates collecting with men:

> So the old man collected the young woman; it could not have been the other way around. Collecting is both a sociable and a piratical activity. Women are reared not to feel competent at or gratified by the questing, the competing, the outbidding (as distinct from large-scale acquiring) demands. The great

> collectors are not women, any more than are the great joke tellers. Collecting, like telling jokes, implies belonging to the world in which already-made objects circulate, are competed for, are transmitted. It presumes confident, full membership in such a world. Women are trained to be marginal or supporting players in that world, as in many others. To compete for approbation—not to compete as such. (p.138)

The Cavaliere 'is eventually going to sell the best of what he buys—and he does. A gratifying symmetry, that collecting most things requires money but then things collected turn themselves into more money. Though money was the faintly disreputable, necessary product of his passion, collecting was still a virile occupation.' This stems from 'a lordly sense of himself' that very few women could have (p.22).

Collecting has its problems. Collectors who find new categories of object to collect run the risk of finding themselves priced out of the market they have formed by their collecting (p.71). There is a horrid paradox in collecting in any particular category, since 'even if you could be sure that you had every last item, the satisfaction of having it all would eventually, inevitably decay. A complete collection is a dead collection. It has no posterity' (p.72). Earlier the French sociologist Jean Baudrillard in his book *Le Système des objets* (*The System of Objects*) had similarly argued that when a collection was complete then it was dead. Obviously once a collection is complete one is no longer a collector, but merely its owner.

But coming back to Sontag: 'Pleasure is haunted by the phantom of loss.' On the other hand, displaying one's collection is not the same as boasting, since the collector is only the servant of his collection. The collector is obliged to display his passion (p.144). As we shall see, she might be writing about Walter Benjamin here. Indeed happiness regarding what one has acquired and is able to display can enfeeble the collecting mania (p.180). 'Every collector-passion contains within it the fantasy of its own self-destruction' (p.187). 'The Wandering Jew can't be a great collector, except of postage stamps. There are few great collections that could be put on someone's back' (p.201).

'The list is itself a collection, a sublimated collection. One does not actually have to own the things. To know is to have (luckily for those of great means). It is already a claim, a species of possession, to think about them in this form, the form of a list: which is to value them, to rank them, to say they are worth remembering or desiring' (p.202). And on this subject of listing, this is what Spufford wrote when considering the sliding scale relationship between such everyday lists, such as shopping lists, and the literary deployment of lists such as Homer's list of the Greek ships setting out for Troy: 'richer, and a step closer to the complex intentions and complex effects of literature proper, are the catalogues of some sorts of collections. If architecture is frozen music, museums are frozen lists.'[29]

In the introduction to his anthology of lists Spufford wrote: 'My own inclination is to think of [lists] as a rhetorical figure—like hyperbole say, or zeugma—as an essentially humble figure that can be extended indefinitely and still flavour what it is applied to.' Ciaran Carson was a master, perhaps the master, of the rhetorical use of lists. The Belfast-born poet and essayist Carson (1948–2019) was the son of a Catholic postman who, rather than be reduced to a slave of the English language, became fluent in both Irish and Esperanto and used to compose poetry in the lavatory of Belfast's General Post Office. His son had various administrative jobs in Northern Ireland culminating in becoming Traditional Arts Officer for the Northern Ireland Arts Council. Though Ciaran Carson wrote novels and plays, he mostly gained fame as a poet. His poetry and his prose alike were digressive and in both he made use of the long line.

THE STAR FACTORY is a combination of childhood memoir and psychogeographic evocation of a vanished and labyrinthine Belfast, with many etymological essays inserted, as well as extended quotations from old reference books and curious folkloric tales told to the author by his father.[30] Early on in the book Carson considered the nature of collecting in general. One of the things he collected as a boy was car numbers. (I used to do the same myself. What did we think we were doing?) But Carson also knew a boy who collected house numbers. Then Carson went on to list things which might be and were collected: 'Cigarette cards, bubble-gum wrappers, barbed wire, spark-plugs, hock, anything in the shape of a pig, gold ingots, pewter, traffic cones beer cans, hypodermic syringes, clocks, rugs.' Fifty-two more categories of collectables complete this great list. In Italo Calvino's opening to *A Collection of Sand*, in the course of explaining the title of his volume of essays, he provided a similar though shorter list of collectables:

> In a recent Paris exhibition about bizarre collections—collections of cowbells, bingo games, bottle-tops, terracotta whistles, train-tickets, spinning-tops, toilet-paper packaging, collaborators' badges during the German occupation, embalmed frogs—the case with the collection of sand was the least showy but also the most mysterious, the one that seemed to have most things to say, even through the opaque silence imprisoned behind the glass of jars.[31]

I recently read a newspaper article about a man who collected shopping lists. Frederick William I of Prussia (1688–1740) collected a regiment of giant soldiers. He also acquired women in the hope of breeding giants.

Though neither stamps nor giants were in Carson's long list of collectables, in the pages that followed he immediately turned to stamps in order to provide examples of subsets in which the collector may choose to specialise in if he continues with his hobby. 'Within the vast realm of postage stamps, for example, one might make a thematic collection, like the simple concept of a "stamp menagerie", which could include the Cod of Newfoundland, the Tapir of the State of North Borneo, the Gom-Pauw of South-West Africa, and the Pigmy Hippo of Liberia.' Carson then proceeds to list the contents of the room in which he is writing.[32]

The book's themes follow one another in a somewhat arbitrarily linked daisy-chain of memory. A couple of chapters later, in 'The General Post Office', he returns to the subject of stamp collecting and he starts with his graduation from 'stamp collector' to 'philatelist'. Philately 'implies study, the classification and taxonomy of minutiae, of variations in dies, fonts, paper, watermarks and perforations; in this Lilliputian world, flaws and errors are as eagerly sought after as genetic mutations by microbiologists, or quarks by physicists'. Carson goes on to quote Walter Benjamin on the overwhelming interest of overprinted stamps as 'graphic cellular tissue'. In time Carson learnt to treat stamps with the attention, delicacy and respect which they deserved and he ordered the right sorts of things from Stanley Gibbons Ltd, 'the Vatican of the philatelic world'. At the same time he became increasingly specialised. At first, drawn to 'the sober, typographical designs and regal, defunct profiles' (in a word, surely, their dullness), he collected stamps of the British Empire. But this was far too broad a category. Then he confined himself to Great Britain and Ireland and, later yet, to Ireland alone. The variations in the first overprints of the Provisional Government of Ireland (1922) were particularly fascinating (pp.30–34).

After a brisk account of some Irish commemoratives comes one of his typical digressions: 'The commemoratives of 1941, the 25th anniversary of the Easter Rising provide an interesting ideological detour.' Carson seems eerily mesmerised by one stamp, known as 'The Gunman', which depicts a Volunteer rebel who carries a gun:

> Banal, pious, badly drawn, next to worthless in monetary terms, the Gunman is not a beautiful stamp, but it fascinates me. I love blue-black ink that seems to have a tint of bottle-green in it, so that it summons up the dull enamelled frames of Royal Ulster Constabulary bicycles, armed with upright handlebars, three-speed Sturmey-Archer thumbswitch gears, stirrup breaks and faltering hub dynamo lamps; the colour of gunpowder, broken states or magnets; the ooze-blue clay of the Lagan at low tide; coke-smoke from the Gasworks; livid, lobster-blue; rubber bullets, purple cobblestones, a smear of rotting blackberries, cinder-paths at dusk, when no one walks on them; the black arm-band of a temporary postal worker. (pp.36–7)

In this manner the banal, miniature image has summoned up clouds of memory. An account of how the Easter Rising of 1916 was commemorated in later postal issues segues easily into account of the Easter Rising itself and the death of Patrick Pearse (pp.34–9).

Other lists follow throughout the memoir, including one of the types of Belfast snacks and sandwiches, another of kinds of female linen worker, another of the remembered sequence of shop-fronts on the Falls Road and another of the component parts of a Meccano windmill. Towards the end of the book he returns to the Belfast General Post Office where he used to find temporary work on the Christmas post, and he lists the colours of the stamps on the letters that passed through his hands: 'agate, bistre, carmine, deep blue, plum, purple, lilac, dull vermillion, milky blue, pale buff'. Carson's list goes on, before giving way to his memories of the Irish Republic's first airmail issues. These featured the Angel Victor, Messenger of St Patrick, carrying the inscription 'Vox Hiberniae' as it flew over rural Irish landscapes, and the summoning up of this image in turn gives way to Carson's fantasy of the same angel with his 'aerial Dresden vision' flying over a Belfast that is no more: 'two-up, one-down terraced houses, shipyards, spinning mills, tobacco manufactories, tram depots . . . ' The list goes on, 'much of it banished now, into the maw of time, but still remnant in the memory of denizens and pilgrims like myself, and still extant in my father's mind'. This in turn prepares the way for the boy's final memory which is of the return of his father from his postal round (pp.289–92).

The book is a marvel. How can any man have had so many words, Irish as well as English, at his command? Carson used his mastery of those vocabularies to take off into flights of etymological fantasy and he chose to celebrate the very ordinary in a high-flown rhetoric. *The Star Factory* is simultaneously an exploration of the labyrinth of memory, a taxonomy of minutiae and the conjuring up of the topography of a city that has mostly ceased to exist. Belfast was once the fifth-greatest industrial city in the world. The abandoned shipyards and mills mutely testify to what it has since lost. Much of the remembered Belfast has been destroyed, either by the IRA or by the inevitable ravages of time, and in this respect, as well as the penchant for digressive fantasy, *The Star Factory* somewhat resembles Louis Aragon's *Le Paysan de Paris*, which commemorated a shopping arcade that was due to be demolished.

SHORTLISTED FOR the Booker Prize, *Shamrock Tea* is another of Carson's strange fictions—not exactly a novel, more a series of overlapping stories. The titles of its 101 short chapters are those of colours and their shades. Jan van Eyck's painting, *Arnolfini Portrait*, is among those objects minutely scrutinised by visionary people who have consumed an Irish drug known as shamrock tea. Sherlock Holmes, a gardener called Wittgenstein and various saints make repeated appearances in the fragmentary narrative—and so do stamps. The young Berenice is admired by the narrator. 'She was like a boy in many respects, and her stamp collection contained many beautiful items: I think especially of her complete set, together with some typographical variations, of the first Irish Provisional issues, which consisted of overprinted British stamps, and the rare Holy year error of 18 September 1933 in which the Adoration of the Cross is printed upside down.' September 18 happens to be the Saint's Day of Joseph of Copertino and the above has served as a philatelic prelude to an account of the miraculous levitations of the flying monk.[33]

Serendipity, the faculty of making chance discoveries by accident, is one of the themes of *Shamrock Tea*. 'Serendip' was an old word for Sri Lanka, and 'serendipity' derives from a story by Horace Walpole, 'The Three Princes of Serendip', in which the three brothers make lucky deductions or discoveries. An early version of Walpole's fairy story was known in ancient India and subsequently circulated in medieval Jewish, Arabic Persian and Turkish versions. The deductive model of the European version 'holds an influential position in the development of "the making of retrospective predictions" that is not only a pivotal feature of detective novels à la Sherlock Holmes but also common to a variety of historical disciplines'.[34] This sort of story may have had its origin in the yarning of huntsmen.

In a much later chapter of *Shamrock Tea*, featuring Berenice, her cousin Carson and Maurice Maeterlinck, the Belgian who won the Nobel Prize for Literature, Maeterlinck compares the three of them to the three princes of Serendip, 'who have the gift of making discoveries of things that we are not in quest of', before going on to recall that Serendip was the old name for Ceylon (now Sri Lanka) and that in more recent times the stamps of British Ceylon displayed coconuts. 'The study of stamps gives us an insight into a wider world.' The coconut under the crowned head of George V is both symbol of imperial wealth and a form of shamrock tea.[35]

TO RETURN AT LAST to Sontag's meditations on collectors and collecting, collectors are discriminating in their acquisitions. The items they will buy should be perfect. 'The soul of the lover is the opposite of the collector's. The defect or blemish is part of the charm. A lover is never a sceptic.'[36] (For example, though the Cavaliere's wife becomes very fat, this does nothing to diminish the hero's passion for her.)

The Volcano Lover ends in an abrupt tour de force, as Sontag (a fervent socialist) abandons the detached narrative voice and hands over the final pages to the republican revolutionary Neapolitan, Eleonora de Fonseca Pimentel, and lets her address the reader directly. 'It was splendid only for the rich, it was gratifying only if one did not reflect on the lives of the poor' (p.417). (But thanks to Sontag's foregoing narrative we can indeed imagine the splendour and the poverty.) Eleonora denounces Sir William Hamilton as a worthless dilettante 'enjoying the many opportunities afforded in a poor corrupt and interesting country to pilfer the art and make a living out of it and to get himself known as a connoisseur' (p.418). That man created nothing and never had an original thought in his life. Eleonora's curse brings *The Volcano Lover* to an end: 'They thought they were civilized. They were despicable. Damn them all.' Even so, Sontag wrote the book in a three-year-long 'delirium of pleasure'.

Now, returning to Walter Benjamin, he liked to display what he had collected, put them in his visitors' hands and talk about those objects.[37] 'It was the small things that attracted him most,' according to Scholem. 'He loved old toys, postage stamps, picture postcards, and such playful miniaturisations of reality as the winter world inside a glass globe that snows when it is shaken.' Moreover, as Sontag noted, 'To miniaturize is to make portable—the ideal form of possessing for a wanderer or a refugee.'[38] And Benjamin was a wanderer, moving from Frankfurt to Paris, to Moscow, to Heidelberg, to Ibiza, to Nice, to San Remo and to Paris again in 1932. In the course of the 1930s he wrote several versions of *Berlin Childhood around 1930*, which is not so much a fully fleshed memoir as a series of reflections on things and places in his boyhood. Finally in 1940 he attempted to flee from Vichy France and the Gestapo by crossing into Spain, but, when the

Spanish authorities intercepted his group and threatened to return him to France, he committed suicide.

Benjamin's most famous essay is 'Das Kunstwerk im Zeitalter seiner technischen Reproduzierbarkeit' ('The Work of Art in the Age of Mechanical Reproduction'), which was published in the volume of collected essays *Illuminationen* (*Illuminations*) in 1936. In that essay he argued that works of art were first created in the service of ritual, but in the nineteenth century mass production had eliminated the 'aura' that attached itself to the individually crafted objects. A famous work of art detached from the society which gave it birth, context and meaning, and then miniaturised and mass-reproduced as a postcard or postage stamp, would lose its aura. In such cases technology has destroyed the holy ritual of art. On the other hand, Benjamin thought of collecting as a way of rescuing objects from commodification. Though Benjamin did not remark on this, it is noteworthy that it is hard to confidently identify kitsch objects in the Middle Ages (or to locate scholastic discussions of what kitsch is). It was the coming of the age of mechanical reproduction that made the collecting of kitsch possible. (On the other hand, a medieval collector, assuming such a person existed, would find it very hard to understand the value which modern collectors place upon rarity.)

So, though stamps must be regarded as mass-produced objects, this did not deter Benjamin from collecting them. In the late 1920s or early 1930s he gave a series of talks for children on Berlin radio. One of these was on 'Stamp Scams'.[39] He began by noting the huge sums that stamps could fetch and told how the rarest stamp in the world, the British Guiana magenta, came to pass into the collection of the immensely wealthy Ferrary de La Renotière.

To digress further for a moment on Philipp von Ferrary de La Renotière (1850–1917), he was the son of the Duke and Duchess of Galliera. Though he was of Italian ancestry and later took Austrian nationality, he mostly resided in a splendid mansion in Paris. He started collecting as a boy and then in adulthood he set out to acquire specimens of every stamp that had ever been issued. Though enormously expensive and difficult, this was still just possible when relatively few stamps had been issued. Even so, by 1914, 64,268 values had been registered and catalogued. Ferrary de La Renotière employed two secretaries to administer his collection. The First World War put an end to the collecting. He had hoped to leave his entire collection to a museum in Berlin, but after the war the French seized it as war reparations and it was sold off in fourteen great auctions in the 1920s. In his novel *The Stamp Collector*, David Benedictus suggests that the enthusiasm of wealthy and well-connected individuals gave stamp collecting status in its early days.[40] Apart from Ferrary de La Renotière, other examples might include the businessman, politician and first-class cricketer Thomas Tapling (1855–91) and the eccentric philatelist and book collector James Ludovic Lindsay, 26th Earl of Crawford and 9th Earl of Balcarres (1847–1913). The latter started collecting for something to do on his private yacht and came to specialise in the Italian states, the US and Britain. He also built up what was then the largest philatelic library. Later these early grand philatelists were to be joined by King Carol II of Romania, King Farouq of Egypt and King George V. In 1940 Carol II was to flee Romania with one of the world's most valuable stamp collections.

Monarchs and millionaires apart, it was common in the nineteenth century for genteel women to collect stamps. According to *Punch* in 1842 'a new mania has bitten the industriously idle ladies of England . . . They betray more anxiety to treasure up the Queen's heads than Harry the Eighth did to get rid of them.' Miss Adelaide Lucy Fenton of Clifton in Bristol (1824/5–97) was an early philatelist and she wrote various articles, including her paper for the Philatelic Society in 1873, 'The Secret Marks on the Stamps of Peru', and 'The Morality of Postage Stamps' for *The Stamp Collector's Magazine* in 1864.

Stanley Gibbons (1840–1913) and his enthusiasm for trading in stamps and producing first lists and then catalogues may also have had a role in promoting stamp collecting. Gibbons had trained as a chemist in his father's pharmacy and first started trading in stamps in a corner of the pharmacy. His big break came when he bought two sacks full of Cape triangulars from a pair of sailors. The first Gibbons catalogue was published in 1865 and that was the start of the company. He became wealthy and travelled the world. He got married five times, to younger women, four of whom died after only a few years, and suspicions have been expressed that he used his pharmaceutical knowledge to murder them. (The fifth woman outlived him.)

BACK TO BENJAMIN and the text of his broadcast for children. He then went on to discuss forgeries and the forgers' preference for faking stamps with cancellations. Belgians had the worst reputation for producing forgeries—and not just forgeries of their own stamps. Then Benjamin raised the issue of real regimes and bogus regimes, such as those of Bengal, Faridkot and Burma, that produced stamps not for postage, but for sale direct to international collectors. In Germany in the wake of the First World War, stamps could serve as a kind of small currency and it was much easier to forge stamps than bank notes. Benjamin concluded his informative and entertaining essay by presciently wondering if, in an age of increasing mechanisation, one would soon see postmarks stamped on the envelope or parcel to replace adhesive postage stamps.

Collecting and thinking about collecting were Benjamin's enduring passions and in 1931 he published an essay on his collection of books.[41] Of course, Benjamin's life as a nomadic intellectual meant that he was often packing or unpacking his library. In this aphorism-strewn essay, we learn that 'the collector's passion borders on the chaos of memories'. Also, 'there is in the life of a collector a dialectical tension between the poles of disorder and order'. 'The most profound enchantment for the collector is the locking of individual items within a magic circle in which they are fixed as the final thrill of acquisition passes over them.' A collection is 'a magic encyclopedia' and 'ownership is the most intimate connection that one can have with objects'. And (as many others have noted) the resumption of collecting allows the adult to return to a kind of childhood.

In *Einbahnstrasse* (1928; selected translation in English as *One-Way Street*, 1978), a miscellaneous collection of mini-essays and fragmentary observations, he included a slightly bizarre and morbid riff on postage stamps and their postmarks, including the following regarding the collectors of postmarked stamps:

> They confine themselves to the occult part of the stamp. For the postmark is the dark side of stamps . . . no sadistic fantasy can equal the black practice that covers faces with weals, and cleaves the land of entire continents like an earthquake. And the perverse pleasure in contrasting the violated stamp-body with its white lace-garnished tulle dress: the serrated border. The pursuer of postmarks must possess like a detective information on the most notorious post offices, like an archaeologist the art of reconstructing the torsos of the most foreign place-names, and like a cabalist an inventory of dates for an entire century. Stamps bristle with tiny numbers, minute letters, diminutive leaves and eyes. They are graphic cellular tissue . . . But in them life bears always a hint of corruption to signify that it is composed of dead matter. Their portraits and obscene groups are littered with bones and riddled with worms.[42]

Whimsical observations follow concerning the unseen stamps of the planets of our solar system; stamp albums as magic reference-books; the resemblance of the early stamps of the German states to lottery tickets; the dandy and parvenu quality of Turkish piastre stamps; stamps as the visiting cards of the great states which arrive in a child's bedroom and allow the child to study the empires' Lilliputian assemblies, coronations and launches of ships.

In 1937 Benjamin published an essay on the Marxist historian and collector Eduard Fuchs (1870–1940): 'It was the collector who found his way into grey areas—caricature, pornography—where the models of conventional art history sooner or later come to grief.'[43] (Here perhaps he was thinking of his own collecting specialities: books for children and books by the mad.) 'The figure of the collector, which improves on acquaintance, has not often been given its due. One might think that nothing could have offered the romantic story-tellers a more tempting subject. But one looks in vain for the collector, moved by dangerous if domesticated passions, among the characters of Hoffman, Quincey or Nerval' (p.371). In this essay Benjamin also found various grounds for attacking traditional art history: 'What is basically new in the intention finds coherent expression principally where the subject meets it halfway. This happens in the interpretation of iconography, in the consideration of mass art, and in the study of the technology of reproduction' (p.362). According to Benjamin, Fuchs valued anonymity of design as exemplified in Tang tomb furnishings. This 'is an important proof that what we confront here is never the experience of a particular artist, but rather the way the world and things were seen in those days by society at large' (p.384).

In 1932 Benjamin finally left Germany and settled in Paris. But already in 1927 he had begun work on *Das Passagen-Werk* (*The Arcades Project*) and he would continue to work on it until his death. The glass-roofed pedestrian arcades of Parisian shops which dated from the nineteenth century furnished him with his primary 'convolute'. A 'convolute' was, in this context, the word for a section or topic in the great Project. The Project's many convolutes, largely composed of collections of quotations, included Mannequins, Mirrors, Boredom, Baudelaire, Charles Fourier, Conspiracies, the theory of knowledge and the collector. Effectively Benjamin was creating a literary collage. The art form of collage, which features prominently in this book, has been defined as 'a process of construction with found papers and other materials that may be already coloured or imprinted with texts or images . . . collage is the result of a process of assemblage that in itself highlights the break with tradition and redefines the artist as a manipulator of prefabricated forms'.[44]

Benjamin was fascinated by the figure of the *flâneur*, the idler and urban explorer. *Flâneurs* do not rove around the cities in gangs, for the *flâneur* is an essentially solitary figure. 'The city is the realization of the ancient dream of humanity, the labyrinth. It is this reality to which the *flâneur*, without knowing it, devotes himself.'[45] However, according to Naomi Schor, 'collecting, rather more than *flânerie*, is the activity that most closely approximates to that of the author in that collecting and especially (though not exclusively) book-collecting involves the retrieval and ordering of things past; collecting provides the link between the bourgeois childhood evoked in *Berlin Childhood* and the adult project of *Das Passagen-Werk*'. Collected objects trigger memories of the times and places when and where the collected objects were acquired. It is only when the collection gets systematically arranged that seriality takes over from a nostalgia that was based on memories of the time and place of purchase. Cataloguing also imposes seriality on random purchases.[46] Susan Stewart (whom we will come to) also emphasised the importance of seriality in collecting. It would not do to acquire all at once a collection *in toto*.

But prior to an eventual triumph of seriality, a person's collection lies largely in the province of memory:

> Happiness of the collector, happiness of the solitary: tête-à-tête with things. Is not this the felicity that suffuses our memories—that in them we are alone with particular things, which range about us in their silence, and that even the people who haunt our thoughts then partake in this steadfast, confederate silence of things. The collector 'stills' his fate. And that means he disappears in the world of memory.[47]

In *A Collection of Sand* the novelist and essayist Italo Calvino (1923–85) claimed that every collection was also a diary, 'a diary of travels, of course, but also of feelings, states of mind, moods'.[48]

As for Benjamin's convolute of the 'The Collector':

> What is decisive in collecting is that the object is detached from all its original functions in order to enter into the closest conceivable relation to things of the same kind . . . completeness. And for the true collector, every single thing in this system becomes an encyclopedia of all knowledge of the epoch, the landscape, the industry, and the owner from which it comes . . . Collecting is a form of practical memory.[49]

Children and old men collect. 'The collector lives in a piece of dream life.' The collector severs the object from its functional matrix, inserting it in a collage. Marx (whom Benjamin revered without reading) expressed his contempt for the collector's servitude to reification and his idolatry of market fashions. *The Arcades Project* was in itself an example of one of the convolutes which it sought to study, as it was primarily a collection of quotations rather than a fixed argument or narrative. In this respect it rather resembled Warburg's pinboard. Contraposition of things generated ideas.

Digression was as important to Benjamin's thinking and his literary style as it had been for De Quincey before him (and for me today). Digression and interruption were crucial to the shaping of *The Arcades Project*, not betrayals of it. An unbroken narrative would have invalidated what Benjamin was trying to say. The sequence of quotations that he was collecting amounted to a literary montage (and montage was a technique much favoured by the Surrealists). The interruptions were intended to make the reader pause for thought. They were also intended to foreground the present rather than chronological evolution.

There were many aspects to the project and, in part, it was intended to be an exposé of the disastrous arrival of modernity. Paris had been the capital of the nineteenth century *par excellence* and in 'The Collector' convolute Benjamin went on to observe the curious fact that the collector's items were customarily industrially mass-produced. Setting aside the *Wunderkammers* of earlier centuries with their uniquely curious objects, the sort of collecting that interested Benjamin only really began in the nineteenth century. Postage stamps are evidently a mass-produced phenomenon of *modernity*. So was the consequent listing or cataloguing: 'By the nineteenth century—the proverbial great age of things, of confident, prolific materialism—listing as a method of characterisation had become institutionalised in fictional and non-fictional prose.'[50]

'The father of Surrealism was Dada; its mother was an arcade.' Surrealism had a powerful role in shaping Benjamin's project, for the Surrealists saw reality as things. 'The genius of Surrealism was to generalize with ebullient candor the baroque cult of ruins; to perceive that the nihilistic energies of the modern era make everything a ruin or fragment—and therefore collectible. A world whose past has become (by definition) obsolete, and whose present churns out instant antiques, invites custodians, decoders, and collectors.'[51]

Two key Surrealist novels had worked on Benjamin's imagination. The first of these was Aragon's *Le Paysan de Paris*, in which the arcaded Passage de l'Opéra provided the setting for all sorts of Surrealist fantasies. In 1919 Louis Aragon and André Breton, at one in their detestation of Montparnasse and Montmartre, decided to make a café in the Passage de l'Opéra the regular meeting place for the Surrealists and their friends. 'Those shops, hotels, cafés, hairdressers, small brothels, the stamp-dealer and shabby theatre, which make up the double arcades of the Passage de l'Opéra are of nineteenth-century origin, and down at heel.'[52]

But in 1925 the Passage de l'Opéra was scheduled to be demolished to make way for the Boulevard Haussmann. *Le Paysan du Paris*, an extended prose poem published in 1926, would be presented by Aragon as 'a mythology of the modern' in which the marvellous was discovered in the everyday. Yet the novel was also unmistakably a nostalgic lament for what was going to be irretrievably lost. The Passage was a doomed sanctuary of the ephemeral. Besides the stamp dealer's shop already mentioned, the Passage also contained an agency which accepted unstamped postage and then, for a fee, arranged for post to be sent from anywhere in the world with the deceitfully prescribed foreign stamps on the envelope or parcel.[53] For those not particularly interested in philatelic matters, there were many other small shops and some cafés, and Aragon described the Passage as an 'alhambra of whores'. Despite some outright hallucinatory extravagances, including the vision of a mermaid in a shop specialising in the sale of walking sticks, most of the detail is minutely realistic, so that *Le Paysan de Paris* reads like a fevered documentary. In the second part of the novel Aragon left the Passage for another favourite venue of the Surrealists (and of would-be suicides), the Parc des Buttes-Chaumont.

André Breton's *Nadja*, the second novel that had fascinated Benjamin, made use of a more variegated use of Parisian topography.[54] Breton's real-life ten-day tragic affair with Nadja provided the novel with an unreliable narrative thread. Nadja was a pseudonym to protect the identity of the woman in question. She features as a mad prostitute and at the same time a genius loci. Perhaps Breton wrote the book in jealous emulation of *Le Paysan de Paris*. *Nadja* was illustrated with photographs, most of which featured unexciting views of the city. An awful lot of Parisian topography was traversed in this anti(?)-novel. Breton and his associates had little time for the countryside, since city streets were their natural habitat. These streets provided signs, coincidences and enigmatic encounters which gave rise to powerful passions. Certain well-known locations in the city filled Breton and Nadja with dread. Also, the Surrealists found that regular visits to flea-markets and junk shops were valuable sources of *objets trouvés*. The fantastic was to be found precisely in the everyday. Each individual's duty was to live intensely and in doing so make up their own subjective map of Paris.

Benjamin wanted to reproduce objective features of the 'capital of modernity' in dream-like terms. 'Phantasmagoria' is the term applied to dream-like images, but in the nineteenth century this word was also applied to optical illusions, often those produced by magic lanterns and that were likely to be of a bizarre and menacing nature.

Le Paysan de Paris is suffused with Aragon's anticipatory nostalgia for a part of Paris that had yet to vanish. As I read it, I was overcome by my own nostalgia for the Parises that I had known from the 1960s onwards—a palimpsest of memories: the first would-be hippy adventure (with that miserable text, Bunyan's *Pilgrim's Progress*, as my companion), when I lived on bread and slept under railway arches or in a station waiting room; my later transits through the city on my way to and from Algeria and my pilgrimages to a Sufi *zawiya* in the Paris suburb of Ivry-sur-Seine, where the sacred dervish dance was held every Friday and where the maddest of my teachers, the holy fool Sidi Abdallah Faid, presided over the kitchen; the hunts for Algerian mouth tobacco; the later explorations of Surrealist Paris with my wife and the discovery of the Surrealist bookshop Minotaure, as well as the marvellous mock-baroque Musée Grévin, a wax museum with its supplementary hall of mirrors and a small stage on which conjurors would perform, all of which helped fashion my novel *Exquisite Corpse*; then, after that book's film option had been sold, the subsequent visit with the film director Philip Haas to the musée and our exploration of the Parc des Buttes-Chaumont; lunchtime games of pinball in the café across the road from the old Bibliothèque nationale where I was reading Arabic manuscripts; the visits to see my daughter who was studying at the Sorbonne; the lectures I gave at the École des hautes études en sciences sociales, the American University of Paris and the Institut du monde arabe. At the end of it all I turned into a tourist who was mostly looking for a good meal.

To return to Benjamin, *The Arcades Project* was never finished. It is probable that it never could have been finished. In that, it not only resembles Warburg's *Bilderatlas* but also that other great attempt to take stock of modernity and mass production, *Pandaemonium 1660–1866: The Coming of the Machine as Seen by Contemporary Observers* by Humphrey Jennings. (*Pandaemonium* was posthumously and partially published in 1985.) Such fantasy projects carry the seeds of their incompletion within them. As Peter Matussek has observed: 'Now it is in the nature of the dream of a total encyclopedia that it must remain a dream . . . Unfinishablity here is no shortcoming, but rather an added value; it does not diminish, but rather intensifies the memory.'[55] Benjamin wrote of himself: 'I came into the world under the sign of Saturn—the star of slowest revolution, the planet of detours and delays.' It was not in his nature to bring his writings to direct conclusions. Sontag's admiration for Benjamin had been intense and she identified with his obsessions—collecting, ruins, books and fragments and, as for collecting, she judged that he had constructed himself from things he had collected.

Like Benjamin, Roberto Calasso (1941–2021) collected quotations and constructed intellectual collages from them. Calasso was one of Italy's most distinguished writers and thinkers. As a student, under the supervision of Mario Praz and the influence of hashish, Calasso wrote a doctorate on Sir Thomas Browne's theory of hieroglyphs—the idea of a language made up of images that would serve as a secret language. Calasso's research was completed at the Warburg Institute. He eventually co-founded the distinguished Italian publishing house Adelphi in 1971 and became its editorial director. *Le nozze di Cadmo e Armonia* (1988;

The Marriage of Cadmus and Harmony, 1993) is the best known of the books he wrote. He was also well known for his collection of books which included many rarities.

The Marriage of Cadmus and Harmony, a lyrical telling of the story of the gods of ancient Greece, was preceded by the first of Calasso's major publications, *La rovina di Kasch* (1983; *The Ruin of Kasch*, 2018), a wide-ranging historical and literary meditation on the culture of modernity. Though the title refers to what seems to be an African legend apparently collected by the German ethnologist Leo Frobenius in the early twentieth century, much more attention is devoted to the career and emblematic significance of the cardinal, aristocrat and diplomat Charles-Maurice de Talleyrand (1754–1838), who is presented as the first modern man. Much of the book consists of a mosaic of quoted passages. According to Calasso: 'It is always a mosaic, if you will, in which I write page 80, 30, 315 in any given order. And I never know where the final place of what I am writing in the book will be.'[56] But some of the characters, events and quotations in this literary mosaic are invented. Thus, for example, Talleyrand writes a letter to Lucien Leuwen, the eponymous protagonist in a novel by Stendhal.

More generally Calasso brooded on the catastrophe of life after the Industrial Revolution and so it was inevitable that he should interest himself in Benjamin's *Arcades Project*. In *The Ruin of Kasch* Calasso quoted a letter from Benjamin to Scholem in which Benjamin explained that his project, with this 'old, to a certain extent rebellious, half-apocryphal province of my thoughts', drew its tone from his piece on postage stamps in *One-Way Street*.

Benjamin, the enthusiast for postmarks, regarded 'history, as presented by orthodox historians, as a postage stamp without a postmark: "bland in its pristine condition"'. He wanted instead to discover a history of ruins, ruptures and earthquakes.[57]

According to one reviewer of *The Ruin of Kasch*, that book dealt, first, with Talleyrand and, secondly, with everything else. The reviewer was Italo Calvino, the most famous Italian author of fiction and non-fiction in the second half of the twentieth century. I believe his finest novels are, first, the trilogy translated into English as *The Baron in the Trees*, *The Cloven Viscount* and *The Non-Existent Knight* and, secondly, *If on a Winter's Night a Traveller*. In Paris in the 1960s he became associated with the Ouvroir de littérature potentielle (Oulipo), a group dedicated to working within formal constraints in literature and in other fields. One fictional outcome of this was Calvino's *The Castle of Crossed Destinies*, a novel based on and constrained by the layout of some tarot cards. He also produced a short account of the *Codex Seraphinianus*, a lavishly and enigmatically illustrated volume devoted to the artefacts and inhabitants of a weird alternative universe.[58] The *Codex*'s images are unhelpfully accompanied by a script in an unknown and indecipherable language.

Editors liked to send Calvino strange books to review. One such was *The World of Donald Evans*.[59] Calvino's review of this remarkably beautiful book has been translated into English and published as 'Stamps from States of Mind' in Calvino's *A Collection of Sand*. Donald Evans was born in 1945 in New Jersey. He took up stamp collecting at the age of six. Regarding this,

Calvino observed that the 'fascination with stamps always starts in childhood: it is aroused both by a passion for the exotic and by an obsession for systematic classification'.[60] Then Evans started designing and painting his own stamps. At ten he became an obsessive stamp collector as well as starting to design his own stamps, including bogusly old imperforate stamps and a commemorative set for an imaginary queen. Evans mainly collected European and colonial issues. Then, as so many boys do, he put his stamp album aside. He later sold his stamp collection to his father.

In the 1960s he studied architecture before working as an architectural designer. In 1972 he moved to Holland and resumed designing his own stamps. 'Equipped with the capacities and techniques of an adult, he had recovered his childhood.'[61] The production of imaginary stamps became a full-time occupation; there were a number of exhibitions of the sets of stamps he produced and his work received acclaim and found ready purchasers. He moved around Holland before settling in Amsterdam, but in 1977 he was killed by a fire in his flat. A posthumous exhibition of approximately 4,000 stamps from over fifty imaginary countries marked his death.

In the course of his brief and unusual career, he had used watercolour on his imaginary stamps, since according to Evans, watercolour 'has a beauty and a beautiful luminosity and freshness to it, and if you try to labor it to fix something it goes flat and it looks awful. It's really not a medium in which you can lie and cheat and try to fool people. That makes it special' (p.106). He preferred to work from photos. He produced the postal issues of forty-two imaginary countries. His sets of stamps were equipped with imaginary currencies and sometimes he painted the frankings and envelopes. Those stamps, which were supposed to date from an older time, were shown as imperforate. For more modern-looking stamps he would use an old typewriter to hammer out the perforations. Though he announced that he was aiming to produce a 'Catalogue of the World', it was an intensely autobiographical catalogue, for it doubled as a diary of his inner states and occasionally catches at what Calvino called his 'restrained melancholy'. There are so many beautifully miniaturised memorials of private encounters, of visits to small villages and restaurants, 'Without the illusion of stealing them from the flow of time which rapidly transforms stamp series into traces of the past.'[62] Evans was particularly fond of fruit and vegetables, and the state of Mangiare was credited with a postal set of twenty-five fruits and vegetables and, later during the wartime occupation of Mangiare by Antipasti, Antipasti overprints appeared on Mangiare stamps.

The incisive and subtly evocative literary style of the famous cookery-book writer Elizabeth David (1913–92) was claimed by Evans as a strong influence on the visual style of his stamps. Her sensual prose had relied on everyday objects, aubergines, olive oil, pine nuts, pots, pans, knives and market stalls, to evoke memories of youth, sunshine and conversation fuelled by wine. (But is it possible that Evans was also influenced by John Minton's wonderful illustrations to her first two books, *A Book of Mediterranean Food* and *French Country Cooking*?) By the way, Elizabeth David was informally associated with the Warburg Institute and she collected cookery books dating from the seventeenth century onwards, many of which she left to the Warburg library. Just as Warburg worked on the afterlife of Mediterranean antiquity, so David, at first at least, worked on modern culinary survivals of Mediterranean antiquity, most notably in *A Book of Mediterranean Food* (1950). Given that rationing then still prevailed in austere post-war Britain, many readers must have read that book as if it were a work of fantasy. Certainly she wrote about a culinary world that was beginning to disappear even in the Mediterranean lands. Perhaps that book can be seen as an epistemological frame comparable to Warburg's *Bilderatlas*. Though David never collected stamps, nor did she have any interest in them, she did collect kitchen implements as well as old cookery books.

Back to Donald Evans. He also shared Warburg's fascination with zeppelins. According to Evans his 'stamps are a kind of diary or journal . . . It's vicarious travelling for me to a made-up world that I like better than the one I'm in. No catastrophes occur. There are no generals or battles or warplanes on my stamps. The countries are innocent, peaceful, composed.'[63] Given this, it was natural that Evans should choose to make Holland his homeland. 'Holland seemed to Donald Evans a perfect place to be: he liked the small scale of the country: Dutch openness to new ideas coupled with hard-headed practicality: an ongoing tradition in painting of small-scale realism: the high Dutch skies and special light: a national hobby of stamp collecting: and the soft guttural language with all its fond diminutives.'[64] Evans made a study of the Dutch landscape artists and Holland, with its windmills, dykes, canals, poplars and poultry, was recreated in the miniature stamp images of the peaceful fictional realm of Achterdijk (Behind the Dyke). 'In this watery country the rise and fall of the tide marks the rhythm of quiet days.'

When I was a boy I too was aware of the rise and fall of the tide marking out quiet days in Holland, for my family spent part of every summer in the seaside town of Scheveningen and then in my grandfather's great house in Capelle aan den IJssel, not far from Rotterdam. One only had to walk across the road from Schveningen's Grand Hotel to reach the beach, and most of my time in Scheveningen was spent on the beach and in the sea, and over the weeks I developed the fantasy that I had been one of the Sea People that dwelt under the curl of the waves and that one day I would return for good to my life in the sea. As for my grandfather's house, it was right beside the river IJssel and its wine cellar was frequently flooded. There were still bathing machines on the beach at Scheveningen. Some women continued to wear traditional Dutch dress with clogs. A diorama close to the beach showed Scheveningen as it had been in 1881. The town is really a suburb of The Hague and, thanks to frequent trips to its museums with my mother, I became familiar with the paintings of Dutch artists and, through them, with the willow-bordered canals, dykes and polders, as well as the mostly wide grey skies. 'The nature of the landscape itself, the colour, the light, the sky, the openness, the expanse and the details of the towns and villages are leagued together in the weaving of a miraculously consoling and healing spell.'[65]

Ciaran Carson also held Holland in special regard. He listed the subjects of the picture postcards that his father used to receive from a Dutch penfriend:

> *The Mills of Kinderdijk. Fishermen of Volendam. Pier and Bathing Station, Scheveningen. Keukenhof: a Paradise of Flowers. Marken: Folk Dances on the Ice. Cheese Porters at Alkmar. Punt traffic in Gietborn. Dutch Girl. The Ever Present Hazard of the Sea.* We loved the ruled perspective of the dikes, the regimental multi-coloured stripes of tulip fields. Holland was a wondrous place, a made-up land.[66]

The list of postcards featured early on in *Fishing for Amber*, an alphabetically arranged collection of discursive meditations on Dutch culture, Irish fairy tales, Ovid's *Metamorphoses*, optical instruments, storytelling techniques and amber, running from 'Antipodes' to 'Zoetrope'. Dutch traders in stamps make an early appearance as Carson imagines wandering through the labyrinth of Amsterdam and encountering by chance a meeting of philatelists in a little square who are engaged in swapping or selling stamps. Gathered in a scene of deep peace, these men are pros who, with their equipment, 'can spot defective clichés, or minute varieties of die, and detect the various grades of paper, whether wove or laid' (pp.7–8). (Incidentally the same book reveals that the Archangel Gabriel is patron saint of postal services and philatelists (p.348)).

To return briefly to Donald Evans, he had a particular liking for Dutch stamps: 'Since childhood, Donald Evans' favourite real stamps had been early ones engraved with portraits of rulers, such as the old Dutch issues with Queen Wilhelmina on them.'[67] Inevitably I collected Dutch stamps, since my trips to Holland and my array of Dutch relatives made them easy to obtain, even though I found all those portraits of Queen Wilhelmina on the definitives rather dull and the images carried by the commemoratives and other pictorials not much better. This is certainly not the view of David Scott, who in his *European Stamp Design* singled out the postal history of the Dutch as being one of the finest and most inventive in Europe: 'The Dutch, along with the Swiss, have one of the strongest design traditions of any small European country, one that has had an impact far beyond its own borders. The Dutch were the first to relate developments in stamp design to the larger world of industrial creation, architecture, graphics and visual awareness in general.'[68] Again: 'From a design point of view, Dutch stamps remain the most sophisticated in the world and continue to offer the viewer or collector not only deep insight into Dutch history and culture, but also into the scope of modern graphic art' (p.57). A survey of its stamp issues can amount to a study of modern graphic design and Scott has drawn on semiotics to underpin his study of the messages conveyed by Dutch, Swiss, British, Irish and colonial stamp designs.

SEMIOTICS IS the theory of signs, an area which was seriously investigated and effectively founded by Charles Sanders Peirce (1839–1914), an American thinker who also wrote widely on mathematics, science and philosophy. As far as the semiotics was concerned, he posited three categories of signs: icons, indices and symbols. A picture of something is an icon because it resembles what it represents. An index, on the other hand, points to something which is not actually present in the image. There is nevertheless a real connection between the index and what it refers to. What a symbol represents is something that is culturally imposed and that has to be learned, and it will depend on cultural and social convention.

For example, symbols featured prominently in stamps of the Irish Free State in the 1920s, including the harp, the shamrock and the Celtic Cross. Then, turning to Dutch stamps, definitive issue stamps showing the queen's head were iconic, since they carry a representation of the monarch, whereas an indexical definitive Dutch stamp design only announces its country of origin and its face value. (A definitive stamp is a standard stamp, not a commemorative nor an issue aimed specifically at collectors. It is used for normal post and is usually issued to circulate over a number of years.) The typography on a stamp should be classified as symbolic, though it can be played around with, so that it also incorporates an element of the iconic. All genuine stamps have at least an indexical element as they must indicate amount paid and country of origin. (But British stamps are the exception here as, drawing on the originating role of the British in setting up a postal service that made use of stamps, their stamps do not indicate the country of origin.) As Scott argues, definitive issues tend towards sobriety and that is certainly the case with those two examples given above. Commemorative stamps tend to be iconic. In the 1920s commemorative issues and other pictorial stamps were taken over by adherents of De Stijl and other artists committed to broad design issues. De Stijl was a Dutch art movement which simplified compositions and favoured black and white. Among the other artists the most famous was the Dutch-Indonesian Jan Toorop (1858–1928), who, as well as stamps, produced fantastically stylised Symbolist and Art Nouveau paintings. 'The postage stamp is a document of its times,' according to the Dutch photographer, architect and stamp designer Piet Zwart in 1939 in a strikingly austere manifesto:

> It does not primarily pose an aesthetic problem and has nothing in common with a painting. The truly authentic postage stamp is one which displays the attributes of the period from which it comes, constitutes a synthesis of its originating idea and which is produced using contemporary technological methods . . .

> Whether the results are considered beautiful or ugly is of less importance.[69]

In Britain two well-known artists clashed over the issue of what was a well-designed stamp. Edmund Dulac (1882–1953) was born and educated in France, but took British nationality. He was chiefly famous as a book illustrator, particularly of the stories of the *Arabian Nights*. (Though several countries, including Hungary, Ascension Island and Ajman have issued *Arabian Nights* illustrations, none of them appear to have used Dulac's illustrations.) In 1936 he clashed with the sculptor Eric Gill over the merits of the definitive stamps which had been designed and issued to inaugurate the reign of Edward VIII. Their argument about that issue took place in the correspondence pages of *The Times*. The photogravure portrait of the head had been set against a plain background and Gill had praised the design for its simplicity. But Dulac counterclaimed that simplicity was beside the point, for the design was bad and it was the overall harmony of the various elements in the design which mattered. Later he set out his argument that good stamp design should not involve pasted-on pictures like a postcard, but should rather deploy things that had symbolic value. It was almost certainly as a result of this controversy that, following Edward's abdication, Dulac was one of the artists chosen to design the stamps marking the accession of George VI in 1937. This was rapidly followed by a commission to design a stamp to commemorate the coronation and then further commissions. During the Second World War Charles de Gaulle commissioned Dulac to design stamps and bank notes for the Free French colonies. (Other well-known artists who worked on stamps have included Owen Jones, Alphonse Mucha and M.C. Escher.)

Dutch stamps were dull, but perhaps the problem with them was that I did not find them dull enough. I preferred stamps that looked like very old banknotes or ancient seals. Dullness is part of the charm of stamp collecting and the fustian dignity of early Dutch and British stamps has been appropriately paralleled by the dullness of hobby magazine prose. In *Le Paysan de Paris* Louis Aragon described boredom as a 'spectre' and 'an exquisitely beautiful young man who yawns and walks around with a butterfly net to catch goldfish. He carries in his pocket a pedometer, a pair of nail-scissors, a pack of cards, and all sorts of games based on optical illusions. He reads out aloud the wording on posters and signs. He knows the newspapers by heart. He tells stories that nobody laughs at.'[70] Bavarian stamps were duller and I preferred them to the Dutch.

In a nostalgic telescoping of time, from my vantage point in the twenty-first century, I contemplate the schoolboy in the mid-twentieth century who let his imagination rest on the Kingdom of Bavaria in the nineteenth century, a principality whose kings and courtiers sought to preserve venerated medieval rituals and protocols. As Susan Stewart has suggested, 'We "luck into" the collection.'[71] In the 1950s and 1960s it was still possible to find the stamps of Bavaria, Württemberg, Thurn and Taxis and the other German states in job lots of mixed stamps that were sold to junior collectors in corner shops in Scheveningen and elsewhere in Holland. A particular stamp in such a job-lot packet had caught my eye. It was one of a photogravure set first issued in 1914 and this particular three-pfennig brown stamp featured the head of King Ludwig III of Bavaria (1845–1921). Ludwig had a fine white beard and wore a military collar. He looked handsome and romantic. I was gazing on the miniaturised photograph of a prince who looked worthy to feature in a Ruritanian romance of court ceremonial, intrigue, flashing swords and murder. I decided to specialise in Bavarian stamps. Specimens of the extensive photogravure issue were cheap and easy to acquire. Earlier issues were more of a problem. Bavaria, which issued stamps in 1849, was the first of the German states to do so. This was during the reign of Maximilian II (1811–1864). These early stamps indicated their face value by large numerals set within squares frames that declared their value in kreuzers as well as their Bavarian origin. They were very dull-looking, somewhat resembling bank notes or seals, but I liked this antique dullness, which seemed to me preferable to the gaudy catchpenny pictorial stamps of the twentieth century that might be devoted to such subjects as famous tennis players, James Bond films or household pets. I later extended my range of collecting to include the admirably dull-looking issues of Prussia, Thurn and Taxis, Saxony, Württemberg and the other German states. Almost all the other boys I knew collected British and British Empire stamps and this gave me a chance to make some good swaps.

In tandem with my stamp collecting I started to read up on the history of the Bavarian Wittelsbach dynasty. This had an unmistakable Ruritanian feel. The little squares of gummed paper in my album sufficed to conjure up the small kingdom with its fairytale castles, gorgeous ceremonies, officers in frogged and braided uniforms in royal attendance, flashing swords, intrigues, madness and murder. A portal into another world, then. In 1864 Maximilian died and was succeeded by his son Ludwig. In 1867 the numeral stamps were replaced by issues that displayed the arms of Bavaria (blue and white lozenges) supported by two lions. Ludwig had been brought up in Maximilian's fantasy castle of Hohenschwangau and it was King Ludwig II (1845–1886), 'the Swan King', who would commission the fairytale castle of Neuschwanstein in the Bavarian Alps and other glorious fantasy fortresses—architecture as quasi-mystical stage sets. Ludwig was also the extravagant patron of Wagner's music. The castles and such operas as *Tannhäuser* and *Lohengrin* served to conjure up the fancied enchantments of the Middle Ages—Ludwig seems to have imagined himself as a latter-day Lohengrin—and, as the years passed, it became increasingly evident that his imagination was driving him mad. He used to declare that 'I wish to remain an eternal enigma to myself and to others'. In June 1886 he was deposed and placed under close medical supervision in the castle of Lake Starnberg. A day later he and his physician Bernhard von Gudden were found drowned in the lake. It may be that Ludwig in his madness had attacked von Gudden and forced the doctor to join him in the watery grave. Or it may be that they were both murdered. Some details of the autopsy surely suggest the latter. Though Ludwig's brother Otto was next in line to the throne he too was mad. So it was Ludwig's uncle Luitpold who took over as Prince-Regent and in 1911 an issue of stamps featuring his portrait were issued on the occasion of his ninetieth birthday. A year later he was succeeded by his son, who first ruled as Prince-Regent Ludwig before deposing his cousin, mad Otto, and taking the title King Ludwig III in 1913. From 1914 onwards the series featuring his photogravure portrait entered circulation, and it was a brown three-pfennig specimen in this issue which had first attracted my attention when I purchased a small assorted packet of the world's stamps in Scheveningen.

But the Great War that broke out a little later in 1914 brought about the end of the Wittelsbach dynasty and brought socialism, modernity and, later yet, Nazism to Bavaria. The king fled Bavaria. The royal stamps were overprinted first with the legend 'Volkstaat Bayern' and subsequently 'Freistaat Bayern'. In 1920 a dreary run of stamps featuring agricultural images and allegorical figures circulated. But shortly thereafter Bavaria and its postal system was taken over by the regime of Weimar Germany.

Eventually I expanded my collection to cover the other German states, Prussia, Bergedorf, Hanover and so on, but, as my collection grew, I reluctantly became aware that some of the stamps I would need to acquire in order to complete such a collection were so rare and expensive that they would require me to become a millionaire. I was not optimistic about my prospects of doing this and so I gave up collecting the German states and then I gave up stamp collecting.

One final thing. Sometime in the 1940s or early 1950s the Surrealist artist Joseph Cornell (on whom see below) devoted one of his boxes to *The Life of King Ludwig II of Bavaria*, now in the Philadelphia Museum of Art. This box contains 'among many other things, a bound book, a folio of photographic reproductions, glass miniature swans, broken glassware and crockery shards with swan images, and two swan bones—all relics of the king's passion for these legendary birds'.

But all that is by the way and, to get back to *The World of Donald Evans*, this book was also reviewed by the travel writer and novelist Bruce Chatwin (1940–1989).[72] Chatwin noted the austere and tranquil attraction of those stamps. He also remarked how in style the designs of the stamps of Evans 'more or less resemble "colonial" stamps of the late nineteenth century'. With a reed pen, Evans painted what Chatwin described as 'a luminous world—a kind of Baudelairean *pays de Cocagne*—that would, nevertheless, mirror his own life and the life of his times'.[73] Evans miniaturised his dreams of exotic places, so that the exotic region of Ajudani, with its dhows, falcons, camels, ancient ruins and Arabic numerals, took its place beside the serene landscapes of Achterdijk.

As a boy, Chatwin collected stamps. As a young man he worked in Sotheby's, rising from employment as a porter to becoming director of the Impressionist Art Department. Then he left to study archaeology at the University of Edinburgh, though without taking the degree. Later he worked as a journalist as well as publishing travel writing and several novels. It is the last of his four novels, *Utz*, published in 1988, that should interest us here, for the eponymous Utz, an aristocratic resident of Communist Prague, is a fanatical collector of Meissen porcelain. The novel opens with Utz's funeral and the jackdaws wheeling overhead.

The narrator had encountered the nondescript and retiring Utz a few years earlier when he had first arrived in Prague. His original intention had been to research Rudolf II of Hapsburg and his flamboyantly eccentric collection, a sort of *Wunderkammer* of curious objects which might serve as the object of a study of the psychology or psychopathology of collecting. But instead the narrator becomes fascinated by the dull and reticent Utz. This man would be allowed to leave Czechoslovakia for the West, but only at the cost of abandoning his collection, and that he could not contemplate. Yet in the end he destroys every piece. Perhaps he despaired of the death-grip that his collection held over him. Or perhaps the porcelain was smashed because so much pointless effort had been expended in trying to conserve the irretrievable elegance of a vanished Europe. '"Wars, pogroms and revolutions," he used to say, "offer excellent opportunities for the collector".' But 'the wit, the charm, the gallantry, the heartlessness and light hearted gaiety—before they were swept away by revolution and the tramp of armies cannot be revived and neither can the delicate elegance of Meissen ware, but only collected'. Chatwin said that this novel was about art, but added: 'Art is never enough. Art always lets you down.' A year after the publication of this very short fiction, Chatwin died of an AIDS-related illness.

Utz is a novel about collecting. Aragon's *Paysan de Paris* is a novel in which a stamp shop and its contents feature prominently. The colonialist imagery of stamps is touched on in Naipaul's *A Bend in the River*. As we shall soon see, stamps and stamp collecting have a role to play in quite a number of novels. Yet it would be absurd to claim that there is an actual genre of fiction devoted to stamp collecting. Rather, the stamps may function as props or as plot movers, in much the same way as cigarettes, wills, clocks, cameras, guitars and magic rings can do. As Spufford has suggested, the accumulation of objects and their naming in lists may achieve rhetorical effects. (See below for José Saramago's novel *Todos os nomes* (*All the Names*) and its rhetorical listing of things that may be collected, that listing being in itself a collection.) Catalogues feed upon collections:

> A catalogue of a collection describes its objects so that they may be imagined as nearly as possible in the absence of the objects themselves, for a practical purpose; by doing so offers them to multiple interpretations, to impractical delight in what goes next to what . . . Something expressive and strangely articulated can be discovered against the functional grain of the catalogue perhaps, yet without eccentricity or opportunism.[74]

SILENT, PASSIONLESS and not expecting to be noticed, objects can be implacable in their direction of story lines. They may also help establish a person's identity and, for example, a grown man's possession of a stamp album may suggest that he is a bit of a bore. As for the plot-moving aspect, stamps are like heroin or cocaine in that a stamp collection can be low in bulk but high in value and therefore something to be smuggled and fought over. As one novel has it: 'Weight for weight they are worth more than anything in the world. Much more than gold or platinum. More than plutonium.'[75] Then again, stamp collections may serve as metaphorical portals offering the possibility of passing through into an alternative world or an otherwise lost past. As we shall see, the stamp album in the fiction of Bruno Schulz is an example of a kind of portal. Though stamps mostly play quite minor roles in novels, it is sometimes useful to focus on things that are marginal to the story. Whether the objects—cigarettes, umbrellas, Kalashnikovs or stamps—have or have not been carelessly deployed, and perhaps conjured up only to be forgotten about, may tell us more about the author than swathes of passionate and high-spoken dialogue.

We will start with the example of a portal. 'Where is truth to shelter, where is it to find asylum if not in a place where nobody is looking for it . . . stamp albums?' Bruno Schulz (1892–1942), a Polish Jew, was born in Drohobycz in Galicia, a small town which at the time of his birth was part of the Austro-Hungarian Empire. Schulz was twenty-six when that empire fell apart and Drohobych is now part of Ukraine. He eventually became an art teacher at the town's secondary school. It was reported that during the Nazi occupation he was shot dead by a member of the Gestapo. He had published little—just two bizarre yet quasi-autobiographical collections of short stories, *Sklepy cynamonowe* (1934; *Street of the Crocodiles*) and *Sanatorium Pod Klepsydrą* (1937; *Sanatorium under the Sign of the Hourglass*). It is the latter, which was translated into English by Celina Wieniewska, which concerns us here.

'Spring', the third of the stories in this collection, is like the rest of them suffused with a sense of doom and dread, which yet is undercut by moments of manic comedy. It describes a child's memories and fantasies during the coming of spring in a small Galician town, a spring which carries promises of strange excitements. The logic of dreams will dictate what happens. The first of these is his first sighting of the poised and beautiful young girl, Bianca. (But she seems to prefer books to men.) The second comes when a school friend, Rudolph, produces a pocket-sized stamp album. It was this stamp album which was to be the fulfilment of hints made by the changing light, the breezes and the rustlings of early spring. The album showed him the world: 'In it were strange abbreviations and formulae, recipes for civilizations, handy amulets that allowed one to hold his thumb and finger between the essence of climates and provinces. These were bank drafts on empires and republics, on archipelagos and continents. Emperors and usurpers, conquerors and dictators could not possess anything greater.'[76]

Then: 'What attraction, dear reader, has a postage stamp for you? What do you make of the profile of Emperor Franz Joseph with his bald patch ultimate within the bounds of possibility, the guarantee of unpassable frontiers within which the world is enclosed once and for all?' (p.33). Here Schulz is referring to the dreary-looking pre-1918 Austro-Hungarian stamps featuring the authoritarian profile of the emperor. But Rudolph's stamp album opens up new and limitless possibilities: 'I opened it, and the glamour of colourful worlds, of becalmed spaces, spread before me. God walked through it, page after page, pulling behind Him a train woven from all the zones and climates. Canada, Honduras, Nicaragua, Abracadabra, Hipporbundia' (p.34). God wished to dazzle him with the richness and variety of his creation. By contrast the stamp of Franz Joseph had become 'small, unimportant, and gray'. Rudolph is its guardian, but the mystical meaning of that album really belongs to his companion who watches the colourful parade of stamps silently march past. Only the spring's birdsong, rustlings and 'murmur of a darkening sky' can be heard (p.38).

There is also the serene and graceful Bianca to be admired from a distance. She is mysteriously linked to the stamp album whose 'text is full of cross-references and allusions. But all the lines converge towards Bianca.' 'A stamp-album is a universal book, a compendium of knowledge about everything human' (pp.39–40, 48). The album also serves as a commentary on the changing moods of spring. Rudolph is fiercely reluctant to believe that his stamp album can possibly contain so much wonder. But the reader should understand that the stamp album is a lightly disguised manifestation of a key cabalistic text, the *Zohar*, in Hebrew, the 'Radiant'. This compendium of mystical texts originated in thirteenth-century Spain. According to Gershom Scholem:

> The explanations in the book revolve round two poles—one consisting of the mysteries of the world of the *Sefirot* [Emanations of the Infinite] that constitute the life of the Divine, which is also reflected in many symbols in the created world; and the other of the situation of the Jew and his fate both in this world and in the world of souls.[77]

The stamp album has served its purpose in initiating the narrator and the reader into small-town life during a bizarre and highly coloured spring. Thereafter the confusing and phantasmagorical narrative, driven on by its baroque dream logic, concerns a group of cavorting waxworks, Franz Joseph's plot to have his brother Maximilian killed in Mexico, the downfall of the Hapsburgs, the narrator's discovery of Bianca's inner rottenness, his surrender of Bianca to Rudolph, and much else.

The stamp album conjured up by Schulz is a portal to the mysterious universe, but in other novels it has become the narrow focus of a deathbed obsession. Benedictus's *The Stamp Collector* is one of these and we shall come back to it. Another is Iris Murdoch's *Bruno's Dream*, her thirteenth novel, first published in 1969. When it was reissued as a Vintage Classic in 2000, I wrote the Introduction.[78] In that Introduction I only briskly mentioned stamps, for I was then far more interested in Bruno's other obsession: spiders. The nonagenarian Bruno is bed-ridden and dying. In the course of the novel an oddly assorted number of younger people perform a sort of emotional and metaphorical *danse macabre* around his bed and more widely in the streets and gardens of

London. Partners switch and switch again. The participants are as follows: Bruno's estranged son, Miles; Miles's wife, Diana; Diana's sister Lisa; Bruno's son-in-law Danby; Bruno's nurse, Adelaide; Bruno's creepy, mystical, hippy male nurse, Nigel; and Nigel's twin brother, Will. The action takes place in London, mostly in the vicinity of Lots Road and the Thames. The novel's title seems to have been lifted from a legend concerning the foundation in the eleventh century of the Carthusian Order by St Bruno who was told by three angels in a dream to go to St Hugh, Bishop of Grenoble, for assistance.

Bruno is not and never really was a proper philatelist, but he is possessive about his stamps. In the first mention of the collection he is fretting about a Post Office Mauritius which has got lost somewhere on the floor.[79] (Post Office Mauritius stamps were issued in 1847 and they are among the rarest stamps in the world. By 2002 the 'Mauritius Blue' was valued at £2,000,000. I do not think that Murdoch realised how rare these stamps were. Even in 1968 the used Mauritius Post Office stamp was catalogued at £11,000 in the Gibbons catalogue.) The thing is that Bruno did not collect his collection. He acquired it in its entirety from his father, who had reluctantly left it to him. The father had strongly disapproved of stamp hinges, though he 'believed strongly in the aesthetic aspect of his hobby, and had often preached to Bruno that a man who did not love looking at his stamps was a tradesman and no true philatelist, he had never kept the stamps in books. He had constructed the large wooden box with a great many narrow drawers within which the stamps were supposed to lie between cellophane covers, which could be fanned out when the drawers were opened. Bruno, however, whose attachment to the stamps was even more purely aesthetic than that of his father, had long ago started to jumble the carefully docketed system by which they were arranged.' Bruno keeps his favourites all jumbled up in a top drawer.

But stamps keep falling to the floor and it might be easy for someone to take advantage of Bruno's carelessness. When Adelaide reveals to Will that Danby reckons that the stamp collection must be worth £20,000, Will presses Adelaide to steal a Cape Colony triangular for him, as he had recently read in a newspaper that a Cape Triangular had fetched £200 and he desperately wants money to buy a new camera (pp.53–4). (In the Gibbons catalogue of the late 1960s there is a wide variety of prices for the Cape triangulars, but at the top of the range a vermillion 4d Cape triangular of 1861 was priced at £2,000.)

Later, when Danby is sent by Bruno to persuade his estranged son Miles to visit him before he dies, Murdoch's novel seems to be about to swerve and become the story of an intrigue concerning an inheritance, like Balzac's *Le Cousin Pons* (see above) or Benedictus's *The Stamp Collector*. Miles wants to know if Danby's visit is really about money and the stamp collection. '"Money?" said Danby. "Good Lord, no!" Or was it? Perhaps after all Bruno just wanted to decide the destiny of the stamps. Damn the stamps, they complicated everything' (p.74). Miles is most uneasy about his forthcoming meeting with his father and he is right to be so. Their eventual encounter ends badly. A little later Adelaide does nerve herself to steal a Cape Triangular. But Bruno soon discovers that this stamp, one of his favourites and worth £200, has gone missing and he becomes extremely agitated. Danby frantically searches the room and insists that Adelaide join him in the search, while the mystically impassive Nigel looks on. Then, while Adelaide is out of the room, he tells Danby that he knows where the stamp is and when he is pressed he reveals that Adelaide took it, so that Will would have the funds for a new camera. Once she is back in the room Adelaide is asked if this is true and she confesses that it is. Then she physically attacks Danby and screams how much she hates him for treating her as a sexual slave (pp.151–5). Danby writes a letter to Will demanding the return of the stamp and this sets Will raging against Danby, Nigel and Adelaide (p.169). Then a semi-delirious Bruno is persuaded that after all the stamp had been found by Danby under the stair carpet. Towards the end of the novel Bruno's house is threatened by the river flooding and Bruno is frantic that the stamps must be saved, but: 'The stamp collection had perished in the flood. The box had evidently floated out of the window. When the water had subsided it was found in the yard, tilted over with some of its drawers missing. The few stamps that remained in the box were completely ruined' (pp.246–7, 250). Their plot-moving purpose has been fulfilled and in the remaining pages Murdoch will explore what it is like to be conscious but close to death through Bruno's increasingly confused yet vivid meditations. Given the complex and improbable interactions in a claustrophobic situation that are characteristic of a Murdoch novel, Bruno's confusion is inevitable.

Though Murdoch was not particularly interested in stamps, she was interested in collections: collections of other objects do feature in such novels as *The Nice and the Good* and *An Accidental Man*. *Bruno's Dream* owes an enormous amount to the writings of Simone Weil and Ludwig Wittgenstein. In my Introduction to Murdoch's book I suggested that a novel 'that was just about levels of awareness, epiphanies of love and self-abnegation and the pursuit of God in a Godless world would be somewhat tiresome. But *Bruno's Dream* is about spiders and stamps, as well as Danby and Diana's passion for the foxtrot, Auntie's crazy claims to be a Russian aristocrat, Will's determination to kill Danby in a duel if he can and the Thames bursting its banks.'[80] All the same, another novelist, Ivy Compton-Burnett, reportedly remarked of Murdoch, 'I do wish that she had not got involved in philosophy. If she had studied domestic science or trained to be a Norland nurse, I'm sure her books would have been much better.'

Again a disastrous end to a stamp collection is one of the concluding incidents in Louise Erdrich's *The Plague of Doves*.[81] Louise Erdrich (b.1954) is half German and half Ojibwe Indian and grew up in North Dakota. *The Plague of Doves* is a tragicomic sequence of stories spread over the decades about a family of Ojibwe-Chipewa Native American Indians and their Indian and non-Indian neighbours in a small and decaying North Dakotan town called Pluto, close to the Canadian border. The novel opens with the eponymous plague of doves which eat and threaten to destroy not only the crops and the chaff but also flowers, apples and leaves. Mooshum, the main narrator's maternal grandfather, tells the story of this poetically beautiful yet menacing plague. Later we will learn how Mooshum barely escaped with his life from a lynching of Indians back in 1911.

Stamps are heralded early on in a quiet way, as we learn that Evelina's father and brother collected stamps 'which was a way of travelling without leaving' (p.28). Then it is mentioned that Evelina's father wants some old stamp albums that belonged to Uncle Octave (p.83). Later, Mooshum, Evelina's grandfather who in childhood survived a racial lynching and who lived on into old age as an alcoholic and great teller of stories, finds himself unable to post letters because he is short of stamps, and Evelina volunteers to get stamps for him (p.192). Her father turned out not to have any talent for banking and, like his Uncle Octave, collected only stamps (p.243). Then when Evelina is over at Aunt Harp's, she receives a call from her father, Edward Harp, who is panicking badly when he discovers that Mooshum has taken several very valuable stamps from his collection and used them on envelopes he has posted off. The father's voice shakes a little. At that moment the doorbell rings and Evelina goes to the door of the aunt's house. The postman at the door has a postage-due letter which Evelina pays for and tucks into her bra before returning to her father on the telephone. She tells him she is now in possession of a letter bearing a one-cent blue stamp featuring a portrait of Benjamin Franklin. The father, whose voice is choked with emotion, promises that, if she can get that stamp back to him, he will send her to Paris, her long-dreamt-of goal. The father continues to be angry as he discovers Mooshum had also stolen a Swedish stamp which was rare. It came back because there was insufficient postage on it, but, happily, a return address. The stamps are soaked off their envelopes and returned to their albums.

But at the end of winter the father, who was driving to Fargo with his collection, hits a patch of black ice and is flung from the car. He is later found unconscious and successfully treated in hospital, but no one had troubled about the stamp albums which were left lying around the car's wreck in the sleeting rain. When the stamps are retrieved it is obvious that they are irretrievably ruined and a great fortune, half a million dollars, has been lost (pp.263–6). We are not finished with sinister aspects of philately. Close to the end of this weirdly and intricately plotted novel we learn in retrospect about what drove Octave to commit suicide in a puddle of water which was only two feet deep. It was his obsession with his stamp collection which he kept in a vault in the bank—worth almost as much money as there was in the entire bank. Eventually most of the collection passed into the hands of Neve Harp, the daughter of Murdo, sister of Edward and niece of Octave, and she has fallen in love with stamps. Anyone who looked inside the albums 'would be enchanted, like me, with the delicacy, the detail and the endless variety, at first. Later you would want to know more about the stamps themselves and the need to know and understand their histories would have taken hold of you.' Then she reveals her discovery that Octave's philatelic interests eventually led 'to what you might call the dark side of stamp collecting'. Octave became interested in collecting very rare errors and from there he 'had gone into disasters—that is, stamps and covers (envelopes or similar materials) that had survived the dreadful occurrences that test and destroy us. These pieces of mail, marked by experience, took their value from the gravity of their condition. They were water stained, tattered, even bloodied, said Neve. Such damage was part of their allure.' (There really are collectors who specialise in disaster covers, mail damaged in air crashes, floods, fires or air crashes, but then sent on.) From these morbid collectables Octave moved on to trying to purchase a message from Pompeii in the year A.D.79 that had been sent just as Vesuvius was erupting. But what finally destroyed him and turned him into an alcoholic wreck was the news that the woman who had purchased the Vesuvius letter for a very high price had inadvertently let her little boy get hold of the letter and, playing with it, he had turned it into dust (pp.300–4). Just a little later Neve looks more carefully at the stamps that remain in her possession and she realises that her brother has taken all the really valuable stamps from her collection, which is consequently worthless. Not only that, she has discovered that Octave was unsuccessfully trying to fake and sell on disaster stamps (p.306). So things conclude with intense disillusionment, old age and darkness.

PHILIP ROTH (1933–2018) grew up in Newark, New Jersey. His earliest fictions were mostly satirical depictions of Jewish life in America, of which the best known is the erotic romp *Portnoy's Complaint* (1969). More novels followed. Much of his fiction has been set in New Jersey, much is semi-autobiographical and much of it is comic. But from the 1990s onwards he produced an impressive sequence of intensely serious novels which, among other things, explored the nature of American identity: *American Pastoral* (1997), *I Married a Communist* (1998), *The Human Stain* (2000) and *The Plot Against America* (2004). It is the last of these novels which concerns us here.

The novel presents an alternative history in which Franklin D. Roosevelt is defeated in the 1940 presidential election by the aviation hero and Nazi sympathiser Charles Lindbergh. Lindbergh has come to power on a platform of keeping out of a war against Hitler which he claims would be an essentially Jewish war. In fiction as in historical fact he was an admirer of Hitler and, in the wake of his fictional assumption of the presidency, the American dream begins to turn into a Jewish nightmare dominated by a rising tide of antisemitism. Yet Roth's narrative is subdued and the slow menace of national and international events are witnessed and poorly understood by a boy who happens to be called Philip Roth and who is seven years old when Lindbergh comes to power. Notwithstanding the grand alternative-history premise to the plot, there is a strong autobiographical theme to this novel, which is to some extent a study of boyhood in Newark, New Jersey, in the 1940s, a study also of boyhood more generally and the inevitable confusions and insecurities of immaturity.

Philip has a stamp collection. It serves as a kind of security blanket. This identification of collecting as some kind of transition to adult afterlife suggestive of anxieties in infanthood is popular with Freudians. According to Muensterberger:

> Child observation shows us that the infant may look to alternative solutions for dealing with the anticipation of vulnerability, of aloneness and anxiety, and often will be looking for a tangible object like comforter, a cushiony doll, or the proverbial security blanket to provide solace which is not, or rather was not forthcoming. Thus, the collector, not unlike the religious believer, assigns power and value to these objects because their presence and possession seems to have a modifying—usually pleasure-giving—function in the owner's mental state.[82]

As we shall see, the stamp album as security blanket also features in Graham Greene's *The Heart of the Matter*, but now, to return to Roth's novel, as long as Philip has his stamp album, it protects his innocence:

> The small magnifying glass—along with an album for twenty-five hundred stamps, a stamp tweezers, a perforation gauge, gummed stamp hinges, and a black rubber dish called a watermark detector—had been a gift from my parents for my seventh

> birthday. For an additional ten cents they'd also bought me a small book of ninety odd pages called *The Stamp Collector's Handbook*, where, under 'How to Start a Stamp Collection', I'd read with fascination this sentence: 'Old business files or private correspondence contain stamps of discontinued issues which are of great value, so if you have any friends living in old houses who have accumulated material of this sort in their attics, try to obtain their old stamped envelopes and wrappers.'[83]

But Philip is living in the wrong neighbourhood and at the wrong time. Shortly before a family trip to Washington he has a dream in which the face of George Washington on his stamps has been replaced by that of Hitler, and the images of other stamps have been defaced by black swastikas on national landmarks (pp.42–3). Philip is allowed to take the stamp collection with him on the trip to Washington. He takes a special interest in his sequence of sixteen stamps showing the heads of successive American presidents and he has a juvenile pride in the historic achievements of the United States. The stamps are a visual treasury of all that is good in the country. On the other hand, he worries that his collection still includes and may be contaminated by the ten-cent airmail stamp commemorating Lindbergh's flight in *The Spirit of St Louis* across the Atlantic in 1927 (p.57). The stamp album protects his innocence, but he in turn must protect the stamp album. This cannot last and later he runs away from home, stealing off by night, but in the confusion of the dark he gets kicked in the head by a horse and when he comes round from his concussion he discovers that the stamp album has gone (pp.233–6). Things will get worse before they get better.

Mervyn Peake's (1911–1968) *Titus Alone*, the third volume in his fantastic Gormenghast trilogy, after *Titus Groan* and *Gormenghast,* was first published in 1959, but then revised in a slightly expanded and much improved edition in 1970. As *Titus Groan* had promised, 'There would be tears and there would be strange laughter. Fierce births and deaths beneath umbrageous ceilings. And dreams and violence, and disenchantment.' Though Peake died in 1968, by the time *Titus Alone* was first published he was too ill from Parkinson's disease to have any part in its editing. In this third novel the young Titus, who is heir to the rambling, gloomy and ritual-ridden castle of Gormenghast after his defeat of the villainous Steerpike, leaves the castle to venture into a wider world.

This wider world is visionary and surrealistic and its denizens do not seem to care for rituals and laws. It is also a world whose inhabitants do not believe in the reality of the castle of Gormenghast. Outside the castle, Titus is repeatedly arrested as a vagrant and threatened with being sent to an institution for young offenders. The magistrate does not take the trial very seriously and he has some difficulty in focusing on what Titus is charged with.

> 'This is the fourth time that I have had you before me at the bar, and as far as I can judge, the whole thing has been a waste of

> time to the Court and nothing but a nuisance to myself. Your answers, when they have been forthcoming, have been either idiotic, nebulous, or fantastic. This cannot be allowed to go on. Your youth is no excuse. Do you like stamps?'
>
> 'Stamps, your worship?'
>
> 'Do you collect them?'
>
> 'No.'
>
> 'A pity. I have a rare collection rotting daily.'[84]

The magistrate would have found a chat about stamp collecting a welcome distraction from the tedious business of the court hearing. Dysfunctional and eccentric, he is part of a world which is much the same.

In the French film *Un crime au Paradis* (dir. by Jean Becker, 2001), a man pretends to have murdered his wife because she has destroyed his stamp collection. Tried for the murder, he comes up before a judge who is also a stamp collector. Freed because of extenuating circumstances, he is then at liberty to set out to murder his wife. Perhaps Titus Groan would have fared better if he had pretended to be a philatelic enthusiast.

DAVID BENEDICTUS was born in 1938 and educated at Eton College, Oxford, and the State University of Iowa. His first novel, *The Fourth of June* (1962) was a steamy book about Eton, bullying and class antagonisms, and was widely reviewed. He has gone on to work in broadcasting and the theatre, as well as publishing twenty-five books, one of which, *Dropping Names*, is an autobiography crammed with anecdotes about encounters with the great, the good and the not-so-good: Danny Kaye, Vanessa Redgrave, Peter Hall, Francis Ford Coppola, Prunella Scales, Martin Amis and so on. *The Stamp Collector*, published in 1994, is a novel which draws on a less glamorous side of the life of Benedictus. Though it is in part an insider's account of collecting and trading in stamps, and indeed the author did deal in stamps at London's Charing Cross Collectors' Market, *The Stamp Collector* is primarily the story of a poisoned legacy and the battle between brother and sister for ownership of their deceased father's stamp album. Though the story is not particularly interesting, the novel is full of authentic stamp lore and suffused with a nostalgia for the ways things used to be in the philatelic world. 'In the early days of stamp-collecting,' Marshall explained, 'due regard was paid to the presentation of a collection. Bound in art cloth on strong bevelled boards, the pages of an album might be of semi-cardpaper, lithographed in the quadrille ground and border, and topped and tailed with marbled endpapers. The whole thing would be leather-bound, as often as not, with a monogram tooled in gold. The albums might then be secured in slipcases. The early Stanley Gibbons "King's Own" albums were objects of distinction, and even the hugely successful Ideal range had its own dignity.'[85] We also learn about the fabulously rare first issue of Mauritius stamps. They are more valuable than gold or platinum. 'Judged by weight, the Mauritius stamps would be worth more than anything in the universe—except possibly the British Guiana stamps' (p.166).

The poet Robert Graves (1895–1985), resident in Majorca, published two deservedly successful novels, *I Claudius* and *Claudius the God*, in 1934 and 1935. The next year he followed those two novels with the much less successful *Antigua, Penny, Puce* (1936). This again is a novel featuring stamps as part of a contested inheritance between siblings, but Benedictus knew about stamps and Graves did not. Moreover, based in Majorca, he was poorly placed to find out how the stamp trade worked and he got a friend to attend several London stamp auctions and take careful notes on how things were done at such events. He also sought advice from a handful of experts at Stanley Gibbons. The outcome was, as W.S. Gilbert might have put it, 'merely corroborative detail intended to give artistic verisimilitude to an otherwise bald and unconvincing narrative'. Taken as a whole, the book has the feel of a piece of middlebrow fiction written for no other purpose than to make some money.

Nicholas Monsarrat (1910–79) produced four novels prior to the Second World War. During the war he served with distinction as an officer in the Royal Naval Volunteer Reserve. In 1946 he entered the diplomatic service. Though his novels are no longer fashionable, he was formerly well known for *The Cruel Sea* (1951) and *The Tribe That Lost Its Head* (1956). The latter novel drew on his experiences as a diplomat, especially in South Africa. Monsarrat had doubts about the speed of decolonisation in Africa and he put those doubts into the mouths of the most sympathetic characters in *The Tribe That Lost Its Head*—decent, hard-working British civil administrators on the (fictional) island dependency of Pharamaul, off the east coast of Africa. In this novel the secretive stamp collection of Sir Elliott Vere-Toombs, K.B.E., Governor and Commander of the Principality of Pharamaul, is used to characterise Vere-Toombs, to advertise the fact that otherwise he has not got much about him. His boring obsession with stamps also serves to remind the reader who he is during his occasional appearances in a novel which is mostly about a savage tribal uprising. The hobby serves as a sort of lapel badge in a novel which is full of inadequately depicted characters.

It is no strain on the brain to follow a middlebrow plot and the reader will usually be firmly told what to think about its protagonists. There are few ambiguities or nuances in their characters. (However, crime and spy novels are often exceptions here.) Emotions run high. There is a tendency for expository prose to tell rather than show what needs to be known. In the wake of the Second World War fast-paced action novels became popular as never before. Hammond Innes, Wilbur Smith and Alistair MacLean were among the beneficiaries, and so was the author of *The Cruel Sea*. Apart from the violence, these writers and their successors, such as Frederick Forsyth, delighted in explaining how things worked—guns, planes, forged passports, bank drafts and so on. One got the impression that this sort of writer knew about such things from direct experience, rather than looking it up in a book or on the internet. All this is disparaging, I know, but, on the other hand, in certain moods I think that Raymond Chandler may have been right: 'Literature is bunk, written by fancy boys, clever-clever darlings, stream-of-consciousness ladies and gents and editorial novelists.'

In Dennis Wheatley's middlebrow supernatural thriller *The Haunting of Toby Jugg*, Toby is paralysed from the waist down as the result of an injury sustained in the Second World War. He is heir to a fortune, but while he is convalescing in Wales he comes to suspect that those who are going through the motions of caring for him are in fact seeking to drive him mad through occult conjurations. His stamp album is used to conceal the diary that he is secretly keeping. It also tells the reader that he is a good egg and that his doctor, who despises stamp collecting, is a bad 'un. In real life Wheatley (1897–1977), the author of spy stories and supernatural romances, was a compulsive collector. He collected rugs, books and stamps: 'In addition to his main collection, kept in safes, he liked to display stamps under glass on table tops. British Empire stamps were a particular favourite, showing Victoria's head on all the territories to which the Empire had brought the benefits of British civilization.'[86]

The famous novelist Graham Greene (1904–91) spent much of the Second World War as an MI6 agent in Sierra Leone. Although Sierra Leone and its capital Freetown are not explicitly identified as the setting for the first of his post-war novels, *The Heart of the Matter* (1948), his memoir, *Ways of Escape* (1980), confirms that this was the case. Like many of Greene's other novels, *The Heart of the Matter* works with middlebrow characters, yet uses them to produce superior literature. When the novel opens, its protagonist, the Assistant Police Commissioner, Major Henry Scobie, has carried out his job with complete integrity for fifteen years and is well respected. But he and his wife, Louise, who are both Catholics, are unhappily married. Religious duty and pity keeps Scobie tied to Louise who is bookish, unattractive and friendless. She is so desperate for a break from the damp heat and the philistinism of their social environment that Scobie reluctantly borrows money from a Syrian criminal in order to send Louise away for a long holiday in South Africa.

While she is away, Scobie assists in the reception of survivors of a submarine torpedoing. Those who have been rescued are in a terrible state, having spent forty days in an open boat with almost no food and water. Among the survivors is a nineteen-year-old woman whose husband was killed during the torpedoing. 'Her arms as thin as a child's lay outside the blanket, and her fingers clasped a book firmly.' The book is identified as a stamp album. 'Scobie always remembered how she was carried into his life on a stretcher grasping a stamp-album with her eyes fast shut.'[87]

Unconscious and severely malnourished, Helen is not beautiful. Yet Scobie is drawn to her case: 'It was the stamp-album and not the face that haunted his memory for no reason that he could understand, and the wedding-ring loose on the finger, as though a child had dressed up' (p.110). Later, when she is convalescing, he visits her and offers to bring her stamps for her album (p.127). A week later he returns with a fine assortment of stamps that he had gathered from acquaintances and he asks her why she collects stamps:

> 'It's an odd thing to do—after sixteen?'
>
> 'I don't know,' Helen Rolt said. 'I don't really collect. I carry them round. I suppose it's habit.' She opened the album and said, 'No, it's not just habit. I do love the things. Do you see this green George V halfpenny stamp? It's the first I ever collected. I steamed it off an envelope and stuck it in a notebook. That's why my father gave me an album. My mother had died, so he gave me a stamp-album.'
>
> She tried to explain more exactly. 'They are like snapshots. They are so portable. People who collect china—they can't carry it around with them. Or books. But you don't have to tear the pages out like you do with snapshots.' (p.142).

At this point, in a rather strained segue, Scobie suggests that tearing a page out always shows the place which has been torn and, following on from that, she should talk about her recently drowned husband in order to exorcise the grief. The theme of the contrast between, on the one hand, a stamp which can be removed from an album page, leaving no trace and, on the other hand, the obvious damage occasioned by the tearing out of a page will resurface at the end of the novel. Helen has found it easy to get over the death of her husband. (When the time comes, will she find it equally easy to survive the death of Scobie?) As they continue talking, a servant enters bearing gin and glasses on a tray. A spot of gin falls on one of the stamps and Scobie says he will get another one to replace it, but she says that he should not bother as she is not a proper collector and she is going to stick the stained stamp in her album anyway. The stain will remind her of this moment in this room. But not necessarily so. '"You can pull a stamp out," she said with a terrible youthful clarity, "and you don't know that it's ever been there."' She assures Scobie that she will never tear out the stamps that he has given her (pp.146–7).

Much later, in the closing pages of *The Heart of the Matter*, Scobie, having decided to commit suicide, visits Helen's place to leave a message. Though she is not there, the door is unlocked and, having entered, he looks for but fails to find a scrap of paper on which he can write something. There is only the stamp album. This must be fate (or a literary game played by a very clever novelist):

> He remembered that particular stamp and how it came to be stained with gin. She will have to tear it out, he thought, but that won't matter: she had told him that you can't see where a stamp has been torn out . . . in a sudden rush of jealousy he lifted up the little green image of George V and wrote in ink beneath it: *I love you*. She can't take that out, he thought with cruelty and disappointment. That's indelible. For a moment he felt as though he had laid a mine for an enemy, but this was no

> enemy. Wasn't he clearing himself out of her path like a piece of dangerous wreckage? (pp.245–6)

Scobie leaves without answering his own question. It seems that he does not want Helen to forget him as easily as she was prepared to forget her first husband, and there may well be a streak of cruelty in his wish to force her to remember him and his suicide. When he first set eyes on her she had seemed so very vulnerable, and yet it is she who will survive, while he is sure that he imminently faces the torments of eternal damnation. Love underpinned by pity for both Louise and Helen has led him to this pass and yet Scobie has no belief that the God of the Catholic faith will show him similar pity or love.

The theme of the stamp as bearer of memory is only one theme among many in a hugely inventive and complicated story which deals with wartime realities, opportunities for corruption in a colonial environment, divided loyalties, necessary compromises, class prejudice, the paradoxes of Christian faith and the corroding effects of heat, damp, sweat, insects and lots of gin. The novel is very funny, but mostly very sad—perhaps the most depressing novel I have ever read.

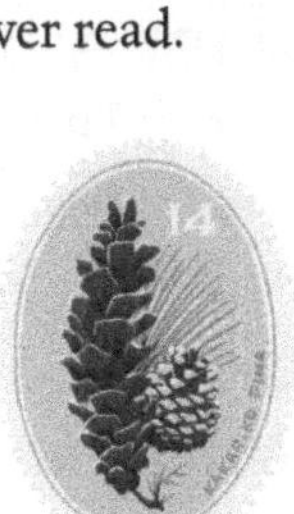

ACCORDING TO *The Chambers Dictionary* 'involute' means 'rolled inwards at the margins'. It is primarily a term used in conchology. But De Quincey gave 'involute' a meaning which was special to him, and he regarded the involute as having great importance in life and literature. In *The Infection of Thomas De Quincey*, John Barrell has described De Quincey's involute as 'an intricately coiled or interwoven manifold'. Yet the manifold is more specific than that. De Quincey's involutes were combinations of concrete objects which, if they recurred in time, summoned up vivid recall of the material circumstances of the first coming together of those objects and their setting. His visual memory of his sister's early death was the key involute that shaped De Quincey's adult sensibility. Having tried to answer the question why deaths encountered in the summer were more intensely experienced than winter deaths, he turned to a more personal matter:

> But in my case there was an even subtler reason why the summer had this intense power of vivifying the spectacle or the thoughts of death. And, recollecting it, often I have been struck with the important truth—that far more of our deepest thoughts and feelings pass to us through perplexed combinations of *concrete* objects, pass to us as *involutes* (if I may coin that word) in compound experiences incapable of being disentangled, than ever reach us *directly*, and in their own abstract shapes.[88]

A good example of an involute features early on in Greene's *The Heart of the Matter*. Wilson, an accountant who has newly arrived in the colony, 'looked without interest in obedience to a stranger's direction, and it seemed to him that no particular interest attached to the squat grey-haired man walking alone up Bond Street. He couldn't tell that this was one of those occasions a man never forgets: a small cicatrice had been made on the memory, a wound that would ache whenever certain things combined—the taste of gin at mid-day, the smell of flowers under a balcony, the clang of corrugated iron, an ugly bird flopping from perch to perch.'[89] As things develop, Wilson will seek to expose the 'squat grey-haired man' (Scobie) as a corrupt officer who has been bought by a Syrian diamond smuggler and at the same time Wilson will seek to seduce Scobie's wife.

In a diary entry for September 1951, John Fowles (1926–2005) wrote as follows: 'Philately. I have been selecting some things for sale. A curiously pure form of collecting, almost collecting as an abstract, pure essence. The only interest I find in it is financial, the romantically high sums attached to little bits of badly printed paper.'[90] Later, less strapped for cash, he was to become a collector of books, postcards and pottery. *The Collector* (1963) was to be the first published novel by Fowles, though he had written most of *The Magus* first and that novel, which was published in 1966, was even more successful than *The Collector*. Other novels followed of which the most notable was *The French Lieutenant's Woman* in 1969. (All three of the novels mentioned here were turned into films.) Fowles was a schoolteacher at the time of the publication of *The Collector*.

Despite its title, *The Collector* is not primarily a novel about collecting. A 1960s novel, it reads like an eccentric counterblast to some of the most successful anti-elite novels of the 1950s, such as *Lucky Jim* and *Room at the Top*. Fowles's novel, which was planned at the same time as a non-fiction collection of aphorisms, *The Aristos* (1964), seems to have been intended as a defence of civilised values and of those members of the upper middle class and above who espoused those values. Although the film version of *The Collector* presented the story as a two-hander, a struggle between Frederick Clegg and his captive Miranda Gray (Terence Stamp and Samantha Eggar), in the book a third character, George Paston (usually referred to by Miranda in her writings as G.P.), despite his featuring only as a series of retrospective regrets on the part of Miranda, is almost as important to the story as Clegg and Miranda. Paston is an older man and an accomplished artist who demands a great deal of himself, for though she is admirable, artistic, sensitive, well read, he is yet more admirable and someone whose high standards she wished to aspire to. Though he features in the novel only in Miranda's wistful memories, his is still a powerful presence. (He is, after all, Fowles's mouthpiece.)

In the first part of *The Collector* everything is seen through Clegg's eyes. His somewhat staccato prose and limited vocabulary suggests a fairly low level of education. He works as a clerk in a city hall and as a hobby he takes up photography. He also collects butterflies which he keeps neatly displayed in narrow drawers. Everything changes when he wins a lot of money on the lottery and he decides to 'collect' a young woman. He prepares meticulously for the kidnap and buys a remote property in the country which has a cellar that can be converted to a secure place of confinement.

His chosen target, Miranda, is an art student living in Hampstead. The kidnap, which is successful, has little or nothing sexual about it. Having captured such a rarity, he does not know what to do with her. 'He's a collector. That's the great *dead* thing in him.'[91]

Miranda, like the butterflies he has collected, is doomed to die. 'You have pinned me in this little room and you can come and gloat over me' (p.45). The butterflies 'are beautiful. But sad' (p.57). When Frederick shows off his skill as a photographer, this too strikes her as something that is life-denying. Miranda judges Clegg the collector as a sort of low-level scientist (and she hates scientists). G.P. had told her that 'collectors were the worst animals of all. He meant art collectors, of course . . . of course, he is right. They're anti-life, anti-art, anti-everything' (p.132). Clegg wants her living-but-dead. Someone intelligent who has been trapped in the world of the stupid. He told her that he was called Ferdinand, but she sees him as Caliban (and of course her name, and his pseudonym, echo those of two of the youthful protagonists in Shakespeare's *The Tempest*). We are allowed to see Clegg (and G.P. and Miranda herself) through Miranda's eyes when he discovers her fragmentary diaries.

Despite the partisanship of Fowles for Miranda Gray and George Paston, there are elements of Clegg in the author's own autobiography. As a youth he had fantasies of holding beautiful women captive so that they would fall in love with him. He also collected butterflies and moths and he loved to take a gun and go out hunting. Much later, when his financial circumstances allowed him to do so, he became a fanatical collector of New Hall chinaware (a line of ceramics produced in the decades following 1810). This was the joy of the hunt as much as anything.

Miranda (and therefore Fowles) harps on the relationship between collecting and death. This is Miranda: 'I am one in a row of specimens. It's when I try to flutter out of line that he hates me. I'm meant to be dead, pinned, always the same, always beautiful. He knows that part of my beauty is being alive, but it's the dead me he wants. He wants me living-but-dead.' In the end, despite himself, he gets what he wants. She falls seriously ill and he does not have the resources to save her from death. Shortly after burying her in the grounds of the cottage, he goes into town and finds himself speculatively eyeing another young woman/specimen. But he is in no hurry . . .

As already noted, at the same time that Fowles worked on *The Collector* and *The Magus*, he was thinking about what might go into *The Aristos*. 'Aristos' is Greek for 'the best' and what he eventually produced was a collection of aphorisms which dealt with the nature of existence and which had been stimulated by the elitist philosophising of Heraclitus. In the preface to the second edition of *The Aristos* Fowles wrote that 'Heraclitus saw mankind divided into a moral and intellectual *élite* (the *aristoi*, the good ones, *not*—this is a later sense—the ones of noble birth) and an unthinking, conforming mass—*hoi polloi*, the many . . . it seems to me that his basic contention is *biologically* irrefutable.'[92] Clearly Miranda had the makings of one of the *aristoi*, whereas Clegg was in most respects one of the *hoi polloi*. Elsewhere in *The Aristos*, Fowles notes that those who possess things are actually owned by what they own. The mania for collecting impoverishes such people in every sense except the economic one.

SYMBOLIST AND MYSTICAL preoccupations and imagery had dominated Russian poetry during the nineteenth century and the opening decade of the twentieth century. But in 1912 Nikolai Gumilev and Sergei Gorodetsky started to promote a new movement, Acmeism (from 'acme', the Greek for 'the highest point'). Acmeism, in reaction to Symbolism, would stress clarity of diction, precision of language and economy of words in poetry, as well as promoting Apollonian values in reaction to the Dionysian raptures of the Symbolists. Osip Mandelstam (1891–1938) was an early recruit to the movement and perhaps the most accomplished of the Acmeist poets. His carefully controlled and somewhat chilly impersonal verses had many admirers among the Tsarist and later Soviet elite. He was a Russian Jew who spent most of his life in St Petersburg. He wrote very little prose and just one longish short story, 'The Egyptian Stamp'.[93] Inevitably the story has collected a substantial critical literature and yet I am not persuaded that any of the critics that I have looked at understands what 'The Egyptian Stamp' is really about. Its content is so private, allusive and disordered. The critics do not even seem to have reached the stage of being baffled by his narrative. (I have reached that stage.) Moreover, I have not found any clear explanation why the story is called 'The Egyptian Stamp'. Daphne M. West's critical monograph, *Mandelstam: The Egyptian Stamp*, does succeed in establishing, on the basis of other writings, that, for Mandelstam, Egypt, like Babylon, stood for modern, soulless monumentality.[94] She went on to find some heavily veiled allusions in the story to the ancient Egyptian gods, allusions often so heavily veiled that one wonders how many readers might pick them up or even if the allusions are really there. Moreover, she sheds no light at all on the significance of the philatelic half of the story's title. At one point West suggests that an Egyptian stamp can easily be destroyed. But elsewhere Egypt with its deathly monuments seems to stand for power. The disorderly plot, if 'plot' is indeed the right word, seems to depend on Mandelstam's reliance on intensely private free association and strained metaphors. But it has been described as a rare example of Russian Surrealism, which seems fair enough.

The protagonist of the skeletal and digressively confusing story, which is set in Petersburg in 1917, is an anti-hero called Parnok. Parnok struggles to regain his overcoat which has been stolen and he fails. Later he struggles to rescue a man from an angry mob and he fails in that too. There are various allusions in 'The Egyptian Stamp' to Gogol's *The Nose* and Dostoevsky's *The Double*, both narratives featuring anti-heroes. But what about the Egyptian stamp? Right at the beginning of the story its narrator asks himself, 'how can I tear myself away from you, dear Egypt of objects?' (p.151). Later, when Mandelstam decides to reveal Parnok's long-standing status as a victim, we learn that Parnok's schoolmates used to call him called him '"sheep," "patent leather hoof," "Egyptian stamp," and other insulting names' (p.165). And then 'Parnok is an Egyptian stamp' (p.166). So 'Egyptian stamp' does not seem to be a flattering term. Prior to 1914 sets of Egyptian stamps in various colours and with various values uniformly displayed a fairly crudely delineated image of a sphinx in front of a couple of pyramids, and it is likely 'Egyptian stamp' was meant to refer to this range of issues, rather than the more variegated historical set of stamps issued in 1914 which included images of Cleopatra, Karnak, a felucca, an Egyptian dam and so forth.

Though clearly disparaging, reference to the Egyptian stamp may also have a different function in another context as it forms part of a range of references to Egyptian and Asian exotica which may suggest that there was an oriental feel to pre-Soviet Petersburg: a Chinaman, Tartar butcher-shops, the Egyptian Bridge, Theban sphinxes, the Chinese theatre, Egyptian gestures, Shiahs, Turkish coffee, Simoom, Arabs, the last Egyptian, Egyptian pap. But then again a great deal of western culture is also on display in this city on the turn: Viennese chairs, Dutch plates, a singer of the Italian school, Washington, Mozart, Balzac, Stendhal, Dutchmen on stilts, Stradivarius violins, the Pitti Palace, Anatole France, Spinoza, a Czech proprietor, a beautiful moustached Greek woman, Barbizon, Chopin's mazurkas, Giorgione. In 1913 Mandelstam had published an essay, 'The Morning of Acmeism', on a yearning for world culture and perhaps Petersburg was seen by him as having embodied this global yearning. But there is one thing more to be said about 'The Egyptian Stamp', though it is so obvious that it hardly needs saying, and that is that Mandelstam's solitary work of prose fiction, with its mystifying collage of images and references, its obscure symbolism and its frenzied diction, must be seen as a kind of Bacchanalian holiday from the controlled, harmonious and rational versifying of the Acmeist poets. There are many obscurities in Mandelstam's life, and his last years are particularly obscure. After composing verses that mocked Stalin, the 'Stalin Epigram', Mandelstam was denounced and exiled to the provinces and later died in obscure circumstances. He seems to have gone mad and either died in a hard-labour camp or on his way to one. It may be that 'The Egyptian Stamp' foreshadowed that ultimate madness.

Molloy similarly seeks to deliver a message which is determinedly obscure. The Irishman Samuel Beckett (1906–1989) was one of the most famous and respected writers of the twentieth century. He settled in France and wrote in both English and French. *Molloy*, published in 1951, was his first full-length novel and, having written it first in French, he only subsequently translated it into English with the assistance of Patrick Bowles. (The English translation with revisions to the text appeared in 1954.) I find it hard to imagine anyone reading *Molloy* for pleasure. The plot (but is it really a plot?) is absurd, bleak and delivered in a delirious staccato. In the first half of the book Molloy introduces himself at some length but there are huge gaps in this introduction. He lives in his mother's room, but is she dead, or what? He keeps writing stuff which every week a man comes round to collect and then returns what Molloy has written with markings on. Then Molloy sets off on crutches into the countryside before acquiring a bicycle and thereafter has various enigmatic and inconclusive adventures.

The second half of the novel is narrated by a private detective, Jacques Moran. At least it seems to be. Moran has been given the task of tracking down Molloy. But why? It has been decided that Moran's son is to come with him on this mission, and before they set out Moran walks in on his son who is surreptitiously picking out his favourite stamps from one of his two albums. As in Roth's *The Plot Against America*, the timid boy may have intended to bring along his favourite stamps as a sort of security blanket. But Moran forbids him to bring the precious stamps with him and decrees that the albums should be left at home, locked in a safe. Is this philatelic incident the crux of the novel? Probably not. In the course of the expedition, while the boy has been sent away to purchase a bicycle, Moran murders a man and hides the body. By the time Moran returns to the house and starts writing, it is beginning to seem possible that Moran is actually

Molloy, or, alternatively, that Moran has composed the narrative about Molloy.

The passage concerning the stamp albums has been subjected to close analysis by an astute literary critic, Phil Baker. The passage is as follows:

> Do you know what he was doing? Transferring to the album of duplicates, from his good collection properly so-called, certain rare and valuable stamps which he was in the habit of gloating over daily and could not bring himself to leave even for a few days. Show me your new Timor, the five reis orange, I said. He hesitated. Show it to me! I cried.[95]

There really is such a stamp issued by the Portuguese colony of Timor in 1895 (and the novel *The Stamp Collector* by Benedictus noted the ugliness of early Portuguese portrait stamps—'an uglier bunch you would not find on any other country's stamps'). Baker suggests that within *Molloy* the stamp is selected to indicate fear, since 'timor' is the Latin for 'fear'. Moreover, Baker contends that throughout the novel things which are not said are just as significant as those which are and, though the image of the five-reis orange stamp is not described, if one looks at a real specimen of the stamp, one sees that the image is that of a pompous man, and this may be an oblique reference to the tyrannical and moustachioed Moran who had given it to his son himself. Though the best stamps have to be left behind, the boy is allowed to bring his album of duplicates along. More generally, the whole novel seethes with duplications of various kinds between Molloy and Moran.

Later Baker returned briefly to the subject of the stamps. In this book he notes that the three authentic stamps which feature in *Molloy* are identified as being from Timor, Togo and Nyasa and through them the tension between the tyrannical Moran father and son is illustrated. The Timor stamp of a moustachioed man (king's head) represents the father—the paternal imago.[96] The small album for duplicates represents the son. Baker identifies Moran senior as an anal retentive. (On Freudian ideas about collecting and anal retention, see above.) A few pages on, after Moran has insisted that the valuable stamps be put away in a safe, he returns to the son's room in order to check that the valuable stamps had not been secretively added to the little album of duplicates and reconsiders taking the album along, before he decides to stick to his previous decision. It is the sort of thing an anally retentive man would do.[97] There is more in Baker's analysis of Moran's nature and its parallels with aspects of Molloy's than is strictly relevant to my narrowly obsessive investigation of the role of stamps and stamp collecting in literature, psychology and philosophy, and so we shall pass on.

IT IS TIME TO CONSIDER the place of stamps in mystery and crime novels. As Ciaran Carson has suggested in *Exchange Place*, a strange novel about the convergence of identities, philatelists, like Sherlock Holmes, have frequent recourse to Bradshaw's railway guide.[98] (This is news to me.) More interestingly he draws attention to Edmond Locard (1877–1966), who became known as the Sherlock Holmes of France. He was a pioneer in forensic science, who established the world's first forensic laboratory. He became a specialist in hunting out minute traces of past contacts and events. 'Every event leaves a trace', was his maxim. 'Sherlock Holmes was the first to recognize the importance of dust, I merely copied his methods.' But Locard was also an enthusiastic philatelist and wrote several books on stamps in which he paid particular attention to forgeries (p. 107).

Robert Louis Stevenson (1850–94) had already written many of his most famous masterpieces, including *The Strange Case of Dr Jekyll and Mr Hyde* and *Kidnapped*, before he finally settled in Samoa, though *The Master of Ballantrae* and the brilliant short story 'The Bottle Imp' were both composed in the South Seas, as was the promising but unfinished *Weir of Hermiston*. *The Wrecker* (1892) is not one of the masterpieces and perhaps it suffered somewhat from the collaboration of Stevenson's stepson, Lloyd Osbourne, in the plotting of the story. It starts sluggishly with an account of Loudon Dodd's youthful studies to become a manager of financial investments or a sculptor, an account that will be largely irrelevant to the gripping mystery story which eventually ensues. The plot is complex, but the essence is as follows. Dodd eventually becomes the partner in a somewhat dodgy enterprise which consists of buying up condemned ships and continuing to use them for transporting goods. At an auction to buy one such ship, the *Flying Scud*, which had been abandoned as no longer seaworthy on Midway, an island in the Hawaiian archipelago, Dodd had expected to acquire the ship with a bid of a few hundred dollars at most, but mysteriously the bidding was pushed up to $50,000, before the mysterious counter-bidder in the room was refused a delay during which he might have been able to seek instructions from the unknown person he was acting for.

Thereafter Loudon and a crew set sail to Midway to find the ship they have purchased. They are excited at the prospect of taking the ship apart as they presume that the bidding contest must have been occasioned by the fact that there will be huge quantities of opium concealed aboard the wreck. They find *Flying Scud*, which is not really a wreck, and take it apart, and, though they find a small quantity of opium concealed in bags of rice, there is nothing like $50,000-worth of anything aboard the ship. So there is the deep mystery.

To continue to be brief, on his return to America, Dodd comes to believe that an English aristocrat called Norris Carthew is behind whatever happened on Midway and he makes his way to Carthew's ancestral home in Stallbridge-Le-Carthew in England. Norris Carthew is not there and the servants are unable or unwilling to tell Dodd where he is. Now, in a short passage that comes late in the novel, Loudon Dodd reveals his (and perhaps Stevenson's) distaste for stamps and stamp collecting as, while he is hunting for clues to Carthew's whereabouts in the great house, Carthew's niece Miss Agnes, a tiresome infant, climbs onto his lap to show Dodd her stamp collection:

> it seemed I was doomed to pass that day in viewing curiosities, and smothering a yawn, I devoted myself once more to tread the well-known round. I fancy Uncle William must have begun the collection himself and tired of it, for the book (to my surprise) was quite respectably filled. There were the varying shades of the English penny, Russians with the coloured heart, old indecipherable Thurn-und-Taxis, obsolete triangular Cape of Good Hopes, Swan Rivers with the Swan, and Guianas with the sailing ship. Upon all these I looked with the eyes of a fish and the spirit of a sheep; I think indeed I was at times asleep.[99]

Then he drops the album on the floor and, as he picks it up, it strikes him how many of the loose duplicates are French stamps and how many of these have different bits of what had to be the same post-mark. When told that the butler also has a stamp collection, Dodd sets about presenting himself as an enthusiastic stamp collector, though 'there is no doubt that the attempt to pass yourself off for a collector falsely creates a precarious situation'. Eventually Dodd is able to piece together and identify the place from which the stamps and the letters which bore them had come as the post town of Barbizon and indeed this is where he succeeds in tracking down Carthew, the leader of a strange and murderous imposture that had been imposed upon the shipping world. This is a case of stamp collections serving as a plot mover. (Carthew and his associates had murdered the crew of the *Flying Scud* and then pretended to be those they had murdered when a rescue ship turned up.)

Though the events that are described as taking place on the island of Midway are powerfully narrated and can be admired as a kind of *Treasure Island* for grown-ups, the novel as a whole feels like a failure, in large part because of the sluggish and seemingly irrelevant start to the story. Yet this seemingly irrelevant opening was deliberate and in the book's epilogue Stevenson actually boasts about it:

> We had long been at once attracted and repelled by that very modern form of the police novel or mystery story, which consists beginning your yarn anywhere but at the beginning, and finishing it anywhere but at the end; attracted by its peculiar interest when done, and the peculiar difficulties which attend its execution; repelled by that appearance of insincerity and shallowness of tone, which seems its inevitable drawback. For the mind of the reader, always bent to pick up clues, receives no impression of reality or life, rather of an airless elaborate mechanism and the book remains enthralling, but insignificant, like a game of chess, not a work of human art. It seemed the cause might lie partly in the abrupt attack; and that if the tale were gradually approached, some of the characters introduced (as it were) beforehand, and the book started in the tone of a novel of manners and experience briefly treated, this defect might be lessened and our mystery seem to inhere in life. The tone of the age, its movement, the mingling of races and classes in the dollar hunt. (pp.404–5)

Stevenson was encouraged in his experiment by his belief that Dickens had followed the same practice in his later novels.

Though the experiment was perhaps worth making, it does not seem to have worked. But let us turn now to an example of just the sort of fiction that Stevenson was complaining of, an airless and elaborate mystery novel whose plot is detached from a more widely imagined world. There are three Ellery Queens, two of them deceased and the third quite imaginary. Ellery Queen was the joint pseudonym of two cousins, Frederic Dannay (1905–82) and Manfred B. Lee (1905–71), and they collaborated as crime writers. They also named their famous fictional detective Ellery Queen. Their first novel, *The Roman Hat*, was published in 1924. The amateur detective is young, dandyish and arrogant. He is also rigorously logical. 'Ellery laughed. "Don't let me dazzle you with my display of mental pyrotechnics."'[100] In the early novels a 'Challenge to the Reader' appears roughly three-quarters of the way through the text and it informs the reader that he now has all the facts that are necessary to solve the crime and that only one solution is possible.

The Chinese Orange Mystery (1934) is one of crime literature's most famous locked-room mysteries. It is set in a New York hotel, wherein resides a wealthy publisher, Donald Kirk, who collects precious stones and Chinese stamps. Early on we are introduced to his secretary, James Osborne, who is toiling over one of Kirk's stamp albums. When another member of staff, Miss Diversey, says that she thought only boys went in for that sort of thing, Osborne gets defensive. Rare stamps can fetch huge sums. Moreover Roosevelt, King George V and the Aga Khan are all collectors.[101] Donald Kirk has one of the finest collections of Chinese stamps in the world. His business partner, Macgowan, collects local posts and, when they next meet, Osborne shows Macgowan a local post error stamp from Nanking featuring the image of a dragon (pp.26–7).

While Kirk is away on other business, an anonymous caller, who does not have an appointment, is asked to wait for Kirk in the office anteroom. The waiting room contains a bowl of Chinese oranges (also known as mandarin oranges). Time passes. When Kirk returns in the company of Ellery Queen, he discovers that the door to the anteroom has been locked or bolted from the inside. The door has to be forced. 'The room looked as if some giant hand plucked it from the building, shaken it like a dice-cup, and flung it back. At first glance it seemed in a state of utter confusion. All the furniture had been moved. There was something wrong with the pictures on the wall. The rug looked odd. The chairs. The table, everything.' All the furniture had been turned upside down or back to front. The corpse of the unknown visitor is on the floor. His skull has been smashed in. Stranger yet, all his clothes were now on backwards and even his jacket had been put on backwards and buttoned up so that the buttons ran the length of his vertebrae (pp.34, 40). As the story proceeds, the reader is introduced to various other things that run backwards, such as Hebrew writing, or, to take a philatelic example, after being challenged by Ellery Queen, Macgowan reveals what he says is a recent purchase and this is a local post stamp from Foochow, one of the Chinese Treaty Ports. But this particular stamp is an example of a rare, indeed perhaps unique error, since the image that should have appeared framed on the front of the stamp has instead been printed on its gummed back (pp.113–14).

In the final chapter the object that the anonymous victim was hoping to sell to Kirk and for which he was murdered is described: 'The stamp on the envelope was a small rectangle of thin tough paper printed in a single colour, bright orange. Within its rectangular border there was a conventionalized coiled dragon. Its denomination was five *candarins*. The printing of the stamp was crude.' This hitherto unknown stamp turns out to be the first stamp ever officially printed in China and, as Kirk and Macgowan make clear, its rarity makes it seem very beautiful to them. Worth tens of thousands of dollars, it was evidently worth killing its bearer for (pp.234–5). Those who wish to know the full solution to mystery should read the book. Though Stevenson would certainly have described it as 'an airless elaborate mechanism'.

TURNING NOW to a very different sort of crime writer, Georges Simenon (1903–89) was born in Belgium, but subsequently lived and wrote in France, America and Switzerland. He was one of the most stupefyingly prolific novelists who ever lived. He published over 200 novels under his own name as well as some under pseudonyms, not all of which may have been identified. He is best known for the Maigret novels, the first of which appeared in 1931. Maigret, a fictional French police detective, relied not so much on 'little grey cells' or on the Sherlockian powers of logical deduction based on minutely careful observation, but rather on Maigret immersing himself in a place, an institution, an atmosphere until he begins to get a sense, perhaps at first vague, of how things must have been and what happened then. (According to Ellery Queen, 'The detective is a prophet looking backwards.' IF the situation and place were such-and-such, what WILL have happened?)

Simenon's *Le Petit Homme d'Arkhangelsk* (*The Little Man from Archangel*) was first published in French in 1957 and the English translation by Nigel Ryan appeared in the same year. Maigret does not feature in this novel. So in a sense the detective has left the author to do the legwork, as Simenon, in an unsystematic exploration, discovers the essence of a small urban community in the region of Berry in northern France. Simenon follows Jonas in his unexciting daily routines and conjures up some of the man's acquaintances and neighbours. Jonas has few needs or expectations. 'The little man from Archangel', an exile from Russia since infancy, has become a small-time second-hand book dealer with an unimpressive shop on the market square. However he has a secretive and much more profitable line of business as an international dealer in rare stamps. As a schoolboy he had started a stamp collection by collecting Russian stamps so that he might find some connection with the country of his birth. But later, he, the foreign, Jewish outsider, came to feel 'guilty, by now, for having amassed this collection, as if were an act of treason towards the people amongst whom he lived'. Previously a marriage had been arranged between Jonas and Gina, an attractive woman who is known by everyone in the neighbourhood to sleep around. The marriage gives Gina a veneer of respectability and Jonas some company. He does not protest when on some nights she goes out and fails to return till the following day. One day Gina is seized by curiosity about the selection of very rare stamps that Jonas keeps in a strongbox in the wardrobe and, when she asks about the figures he is writing down, she is astounded what sums a stamp like the five-cent Trinidad Blue of 1847 and similar rarities can fetch.

One evening she sets out in her sexy red dress but no coat and this time she does not return in the morning. In the course of the following morning various neighbours ask where Gina has got to and Jonas for no good reason blurts out that she has gone to visit a friend in Bourges. Later, seized by suspicion, he opens the strongbox and finds that the packet of the most valuable stamps has gone. He wonders at Gina's naivety about the philatelic world and her failure to realise that some of the provenances of these very rare stamps would be identified by other dealers. As the days pass Jonas becomes aware that the locals suspect him of having murdered Gina. A policeman calls by and asks careful questions. Next he is summoned to the police station to answer more questions. There is no real evidence against him. Finally a woman who works in a nearby hotel tells Jonas that she knows he is innocent and she is prepared to testify to the police that she has seen Gina with her lover in the hotel. It is enough. Jonas hangs himself outside his shop.

Simenon has brooded upon Jonas and the neighbours in Vieux Marché until he has a sense of how things must be and the inevitability of the suicide of Jonas. The unfaithfulness of Gina does not matter. Her theft of the stamps does not matter. What has driven Jonas to kill himself is his sensitivity to the swift and easy rejection of him by the small community of Vieux Marché, by people he thought knew and liked him. But after so many years living among these people he has not earned their liking, still less their respect. He is after all a foreigner, a Jew and a cuckold. Ostracism, not murder, is the subject of the novel. The quest for self-knowledge was a regular theme in Simenon's novels. Jonas learns that the sort of man he is will never gain full acceptance in the little community of Vieux Marché where he has spent so much of his life.

We never learn what happened to the rare stamps. Simenon's presentation of the theft of the stamps and the rumours that Jonas has murdered Gina, have functioned as a MacGuffin, a plot device that sets the story in motion but which turns out not to be the real subject of the story. (Hitchcock's film *Psycho* provides a classic example of a MacGuffin, as in the first part of the film the cinema-goers have been set up to believe that this will essentially be a story about whether a young woman will get away with stealing money from her boss's office. But the real story which starts in the Bates Motel will be stranger and more sinister than that.)

The next novel to be discussed features a stamp and an amateur, almost accidental, detective. Its author Anthony Trollope (1815–82) started out at the age of nineteen as a junior clerk in the London Post Office where he worked for seven years before a serious illness forced him to give up the London job. He subsequently worked for a branch of the Post Office in Ireland where he took pleasure in his roving administrative commissions and the opportunities it gave him for hunting. He published his first novel in 1847 and for a few years a string of largely unsuccessful novels followed. But in the 1850s he moved from place to place in Great Britain setting up the mail system in various regions, as it was being reorganised around the use of pre-paid postage stamps. He and Rowland Hill clashed repeatedly over a variety of administrative issues. Trollope thought Hill was too inhuman and hard on his staff. Hill favoured promotion by merit, whereas Trollope favoured promotion by seniority. Trollope was responsible for recommending the introduction of letter boxes, which saved people the trek to a Post Office. Yet teasingly his novel *He Knew He Was Right* (1869) includes Aunt Stanbury's diatribe against those new-fangled, ugly letter boxes in which post was all too likely to go astray. She declared that any self-respecting person would surely go to the Post Office to send off their mail.

In 1855 Trollope published the first of his successful Barsetshire novels, *The Warden*. In 1858 he went out to Egypt on behalf of the Post Office to organise the replacement of camels by railways for the carting of mail. He anglicised the Egyptian postal service. Showing little interest in the camels, pyramids and fellahin, he found time while in Egypt to write most of *Dr Thorne*, another Barsetshire novel. Great writers seem to have a remarkable ability to ignore the environments they are writing in. Flaubert, bored by his friend Maxime Du Camp's lengthy photographic procedures in front of Egypt's Pharaonic monuments, conceived of a novel about boredom that he ended up setting in Normandy: *Madame Bovary*. Daphne du Maurier wrote *Rebecca* in Alexandria. Although Ronald Firbank had the idea for *The Flower Beneath the Foot* in Algiers, he set that novel in Vienna. But anyway Trollope, who loved travelling, was a ferociously disciplined and prolific writer who confined himself to writing about British society and politics. Eventually in 1867 the success of the Barsetshire series and other novels allowed him to leave the employ of the Post Office and become a full-time writer.

John Caldigate was originally published serially in *Blackwood's Magazine* from April 1878 to June 1879. In part it drew on Trollope's visit to his son in Australia. In the novel, young John Caldigate and his friend Dick set off to prospect for gold in Australia. Euphemia Smith, an adventuress, is also on board the outbound ship and John begins an affair with her. In Australia he and Dick work on a goldmine. After a while Dick, who had been drinking heavily, disappears. John continues at the mine, but eventually he sells his share in it to Tim Crinkett and returns to England a wealthy man. He marries Hester, a young woman whom he had been in love with before he had left England. But he is pursued there by Euphemia and Tim. The villainous pair allege that the mine was actually worked out when John sold his share to Tim and moreover they claim John married Euphemia in New South Wales. John, acknowledging the partial justice of Tim's claim, hands over a large sum of money to Tim and Euphemia, but they nevertheless proceed to have him charged with bigamy. None of the above is of any interest to those who read novels for their philatelic content.

Things only get interesting for such readers in the last quarter of the novel. The chief piece of evidence for John's marriage in Australia is a letter whose envelope is addressed to Mrs Euphemia Caldigate. The date of a postmark on the Australian stamp is clearly legible and the lawyer defending John argues that this is suspicious:

> I shall call before you two gentlemen experienced in the affairs of the post office, and they will tell you that the postmarks on this envelope, both that of the town, Sydney, and that by which the postage stamp is obliterated, are cleaner, finer, and better perceived than they would have been had it passed in the ordinary course through the post office. Letters in the post office are hurried quickly through the operation of stamping, so that

> one passing over the other while he stamping ink is still moist, will to some extent blot and blur that with which it has come in contact. He will produce some dozens taken at random, and will show that with them all such has been the case. This blotting, this smudging, is very slight, but it exists; it is always there. He will tell you that this envelope has been stamped as one and alone—by itself—with peculiar care—and I shall ask you to believe that the impression has been procured by fraud in the Sydney post office.

This must be meat and drink to those who read fiction for nuggets of philatelic minutiae. But the judge, who is not persuaded by the evidence of the smudgy postmark, finds John guilty of bigamy and commits him to prison. Now the author's expertise as a chronicler of office life comes to the fore in the last part of the book. (He took a much more sympathetic view of officials and bureaucracy than did his contemporary, Dickens.) Notwithstanding the guilty verdict delivered in this case, a Post Office clerk called Bagwatch is sure that there is something wrong with that postmark and he continues to study that envelope. Only slowly does he realise that what is more conclusively amiss in the evidence purportedly supplied by this envelope is that the postmark has been applied to a stamp that had not at that time yet been issued in Australia. Therefore the envelope's dating is a product of forgery. He takes his discovery to John's defence counsel who in turn passes it on to the judge and shortly afterwards John receives the queen's pardon and is released from prison and reunited with his wife.

Trollope, who had been a Post Office clerk himself, admitted that he identified with the conscientious Bagwatch.

JOHN UPDIKE'S NOVEL *In the Beauty of the Lilies* (1996) presents the story of four generations of the Wilmot family in the small Delaware town of Basingstoke. In the background of this family chronicle, a history of American cinema from 1910 to 1990 serves as a kind of commentary on the hopes and fears of mostly ordinary American citizens as their country's society and economy evolves. A member of the second generation of Wilmots, Teddy is very ordinary. As a boy he is shy and afraid of any kind of challenge. He prefers to stay in his bedroom and sort out his collections of baseball cards 'or foreign stamps in one of the little sheltering worlds of papery order he tried to make'. He also likes his early morning job delivering newspapers: 'Always he loved this sensation, hard to describe, of *delivering*, and then of moving on. It satisfied the same side of him as arranging stamps on the page.'[102] Teddy 'knew from school that he was cautious and underdeveloped . . . He wasn't equipped, he was still curled inward, collecting innocent things—stamps from foreign countries that gave pieces of paper the power to fly around the globe. The few friends he had at school would give him or sell him for a penny the stamps from their relatives in Europe, even Turkey and Syria, and new countries like Czechoslovakia and Lebanon. The passion of those tiny stamps in the intensity of their colors and engraving and words of unknown languages fascinated him, drew him in, to a small safe cave' (p.131). As an adult he will find emotional safety in becoming one of Basingstoke's postmen. Every weekday he will contentedly follow the same track round the town.

It is just possible that Updike put quite a bit of himself into Teddy. Some ten years earlier, in a panel discussion in New York on January 13, 1986, 'The Writer's Imagination and the Imagination of the State', a session of a PEN International Congress, he had this to say:

> The place where my personal hopes and dreams and the intentions and provisions of the state intersected was the postal system. Its workers, whom in my small town I knew all by name, brought to the house the printed journals—the newspapers and magazines—that represented to me a world where I wished to locate my future. In those days when a postage stamp cost three cents, I sent letters to distant and great men, cartoonists and writers, some of whom deigned to my eternal gratitude to respond. Each day's mail brought potential treasure. This is still true for me. I send manuscripts away, I sometimes get praise and money in return. It is the United States mails with the myriad routes and mechanisms that the service implies, not to mention the basic honesty and efficiency and

> non-interference of its thousands of employees that enable me to live as I do, and to do what I do. I never see a blue mailbox without a spark of warmth and wonder and gratitude that this extensive service is maintained for my benefit.

For Updike stamps are objects, but objects imbued with human intention. He liked to quote the poet William Carlos Williams to the effect that there are 'no ideas but in things'. Many regard Updike (1932–2009) as the greatest American novelist of the second half of the twentieth century and he was also widely rated as a poet and critic. He is best known for the novels *Couples* (1968) and the Rabbit tetralogy: *Rabbit, Run* (1960), *Rabbit Redux* (1971), *Rabbit Is Rich* (1981) and *Rabbit at Rest* (1990). The meticulously evoked ups and downs of the life of Harry (Rabbit) Angstrom uses an account of his rather ordinary career and fleeting moments of sexual happiness to chronicle life in small-town America and through this chronicle to provide a highly critical commentary on American politics and society more broadly.

Sex and eroticism are prominent in all these and others of Updike's novels and poems. They may even colour his feelings for postage stamps. In one of his poems, 'Not Cancelled Yet', which must be about the imminence of death and then about stamps but may be about something else altogether, he fantasises about one day becoming a postage stamp, 'but I won't be there to lick me / and licking was what I liked'. Subsequent references to 'the long dark slither' and 'flickering of fingers' suggest that something other than the US Mail Service is being rhapsodised.[103]

The Argentinian author and novelist Julio Cortázar (1914–84) spent most of his life in Europe. He acquired a reputation as a difficult writer. His short story 'Los venenos' ('Poisons') suggests that he was also a subtle one. The story is set in one of the suburbs of Buenos Aires and it is an evocation of childhood. A child tells the story without realising what the story is and in doing so evokes the poisoning of the paradise of boyhood. One source of poison has been brought to the household by Uncle Carlos: 'It looked like a black iron stove, with three curved legs, a door for the furnace, another for the poison: from the top emerged a tube of metal (like a worm) where we would later insert a rubber tube with a spout.' This strange device will be set working to kill the ants that have been infesting the garden and house by fumigating their tunnels with a poisonous chemical. Consequently ants die in their thousands.

The siesta time is spent indoors and the boy uses this time to sort out his stamp collection and, at the time of the ant-killing machine's inauguration, the boy's best friend, Hugo, has arrived and so during the siesta period the boy rearranges his stamps in the company of Hugo and passes on some of his duplicates to him. Hugo begins to contemplate putting together his own collection, though he said that he would omit certain categories of stamps and that would make his collection more valuable. The boy's sister (who clearly fancies Hugo) agrees, 'even though she wouldn't have been able to tell if a stamp was upside down or the right way up'. Her brother thinks that she just wanted to contradict him. But a little later Lila, the girl next door (whom the boy clearly fancies, even if he is not fully aware of it), drops by and supports the boy's liking for European stamps. He recalls that once he had 'given Lila an envelope with all sorts of different stamps, and she'd always remind me of it, saying that her father was going to help her with the collection but that her mother said that wasn't for girls, stamps were full of germs, and the envelope was kept away in a cupboard'. Later, towards the end of this memoir of a half-started childhood romance, the boy discovers that, before returning home, Hugo had visited Lila to say goodbye and to give her his immensely precious peacock's feather, the feather which he had barely allowed his best friend to touch. The boy takes a displaced kind of vengeance by setting the ugly black machine going so that many more ants will die. Arguably this is a memoir of that sexually labile period which so often seems to herald the abandonment of stamp collecting by boys and the rise of their sexual awareness. But childhood's end has not come yet.[104]

The Portuguese novelist, poet and communist polemicist José Saramago (1922–2010) was awarded the Nobel Prize for Literature in 1998. He was noted for his pessimism and the enigmatic quality of his novels. When *Todos os nomes* was published in Portuguese in 1997 and in English as *All the Names* in 1999, several of the book's reviewers and readers confessed that they were uncertain as to what the book really was about. I was among them.[105] Most of Saramago's chilly bureaucratic fable is set in the Central Registry of Births, Marriages and Deaths of an unknown country. Senhor José works as a subordinate clerk in the Registry. He is the only character in the novel to be distinguished by a personal name. The subordinate clerks do most of the work. The upper reaches of the administration do little except collect information about their subordinates. When José is not working he passes the time by collecting press cuttings of famous people:

> There are people like Senhor José everywhere, who fill their spare time, or what they believe to be their spare time, by collecting stamps, coins, medals, vases, postcards, matchboxes, books, clocks, sports shirts, autographs, stones, clay figurines, empty drinks cans, little angels, cacti, opera programmes, lighters, pens, owls, music boxes, bottles, bonsai trees, paintings, mugs, pipes, glass obelisks, ceramic ducks, old toys, carnival masks, and they probably do so out of something that we might call metaphysical angst, perhaps because they cannot bear the idea of chaos being the one ruler of the universe, which is why, using their limited powers and with no divine help, they attempt to impose some order on the world and for a while they manage it, but only as long as they are there to defend their collection, because when the day comes when it must be dispersed, and that day always comes, either with their death or when the collector grows weary, everything goes back to its beginnings, everything returns to chaos.[106]

In this light the entropy to which every collection must fall victim might be seen as a kind of memento mori directed at the collector. Saramago favoured long sentences with punctuation a rare and regrettable necessity and towards the end of the novel there is an even longer and more impressive list of different types of funeral monuments.

On a dangerous impulse, José sneaks into the Registry Office one night to borrow some file cards of famous people to pad out his collection. But by accident he also carries away the card of an unknown woman and thereafter he becomes obsessed with trying to track down this woman who is not famous at all. As his quest progresses he comes to realise the futility of his collecting press cuttings of the famous—pieces of paper which take no account of the happiness or unhappiness of that select few. At the same time Saramago manages to deliver the strange message for which, I think, his austere parable has served as a vehicle: the dead deserve as much recognition as the living in our society. The novel concludes with the adoption of a new filing system in the labyrinthine Registry in which the records of the living and the dead are to be given equal importance. Although collecting does feature in the novel, it is not really a major theme, but the listing of hobbies taken up from fear of chaos should rather be seen as a high-spirited literary riff, just like the later listing of different kinds of funerary memorial.

Hugh Lofting (1886–1947) wrote and illustrated the Dolittle novels, idiosyncratic stories for children about a doctor who can converse with animals. *The Story of Doctor Dolittle* was the first book in the series in 1922 and *Doctor Dolittle's Post Office* (1924) was the third. As will be the case in Ankh-Morpork (to which we will come shortly), a central Post Office is in bad need of reorganisation as vast heaps of undelivered mail lie around the building.

In this case the Post Office is on the island of Fantipo, 'a savage African kingdom'. While Fantipo's ruler, King Koko, was keen on having his image on the recently invented postage stamp, he had neglected the supervision of the Post Office. But, being a very vain man, 'he had a fine lot of stamps made with his pictures on them, some with his crown on and some without; some smiling, some frowning; some with himself on horseback, some with himself on a bicycle. But the stamp which he was most proud of was the tenpenny stamp which bore a portrait of himself playing golf—a game he had just recently learned from some Scotchmen who were mining for gold in his kingdom.'[107] Once Dolittle gets the postal service up and running again, stamp collecting catches on. 'The King himself became a stamp-collector and his album was as good as a family photo-album, containing as it did so many pictures of himself' (p.213). (One wonders if George V contemplated some of his albums in just the same way.) Lofting's presentation of the reorganisation of an exotic Post Office is a MacGuffin, as it provides some sort of loose narrative thread which allows the presentation of a lot of animal and bird stories which have little or nothing to do with postal matters. Lofting provided the book with his quaintly naïve illustrations, including some of Fantipo's stamps. Subsequently Bruce Grenville (b.1950), the New Zealand artist, anarchist and hoaxer, belatedly produced Fantipo's stamps, the designs of which were closely modelled on Lofting's illustrations. King Koko looks magnificently ugly on the one-penny stamp. (For Grenville's other philatelic work on Upper Yafa and other imaginary places, see below.)

THE COLOUR OF MAGIC by the British fantasy writer Terry Pratchett (1948–2015), which was the first novel in his comic Discworld series, appeared in 1983. Subsequently he published over fifty novels, of which forty-one were set in Discworld. According to David Langford, Discworld 'is a playground where reality is thin and fragile, and where "narrative causality"—the momentum of a story—has shaping power; "morphic resonance" makes Discworld overtly a mirror of our world and its stories . . . a distorting mirror'.[108] As a child Pratchett had collected Brooke Bond Tea Cards about space and much later he has remarked that 'It is easier to bend the universe around the story'. In the twisted universe that he created, the flat circular Discworld rests on the backs of four elephants who in turn stand on the back of a giant turtle. Modern innovations such as guns, cinema, steam engines—and postal services—and their impact on a largely medieval world are often the theme of his novels. Pratchett enjoyed working with clichés, which he was skilled at twisting to give them new meanings. His wordplay is fun, for example 'the smoking gnu' in *Going Postal*. Though his Discworld books are broadly comic fantasy, there is also a fair bit of serious social comment. 'Not everything in a Discworld book is meant to be funny,' according to Pratchett.

The small, obsessive world of the collector is evocatively described in the Discworld novel *Going Postal*.[109] Moist Lipwig started out in life as a confidence trickster. But like Dr Dolittle he has somehow been appointed to reorganise the postal service of Ankh-Morpork. But, unlike Fantipo, the citizens of Ankh-Morpork have no notion of what a postage stamp might be. Prior to Moist's invention of stamps, one of his rather inadequate underlings, Stanley, has been an avid collector of pins. The hobby is known as acuphilia and Stanley goes for a walk to the self-styled 'Home of Acuphilia!!!'

> It was like lifting an unregarded stone and finding a whole new world. Dave's Pin Exchange was the kind of shop where the owner knows every single one of his customers by name. It was a wonderful world, the world of pins. It was a hobby that could last you a lifetime. Moist knew this because he expended one dollar on *Pins* by J. Lanugo Owslbury, apparently the last word on the subject. Everyone had their funny little ways, Moist conceded, but he wasn't entirely at home among people who, if they saw a pin-up, would pay no attention to the pins. Some of the customers browsing the book racks (*Mis-Draws, Double Pointers and Flaws, Pins of Uberwald and Genua, First Steps in Pins, Adventures in Acuphilia* . . .) and staring covetously at the rack of pins laid out under glass had an intensity of expression that frightened him. They looked a bit like Stanley. They were all male. Clearly, women weren't natural 'pinheads'. (p.74)

Later Stanley explains to Moist that the real pleasure in collecting is found not in the expenditure of money:

> for the true pinhead the real pleasure is in the joy of the chase, the pin fairs, the house clearances and, who knows, a casual glint in the gutter that turns out to be a well-preserved Doublefast or an unbroken two-pointer. Well it is said: 'See a pin and pick it up, and all day long you'll have a pin.' (p.114)

But, once Moist and his assistants come up with the invention of little bits of perforated paper with gum on their backs, it does not take Stanley long to say farewell to boring old pin collecting: 'I have put the childish playground of pins right behind me, sir! The world of stamps, which can teach a young man much about history and geography as well as being a healthy, enjoyable, engrossing and thoroughly worthwhile hobby that will give him an interest that will last him a lifetime' (p.398).

In *Zany Afternoons* the whimsical Canadian writer and illustrator Bruce McCall similarly mocked stamp collecting, as in the two-page illustrated layout entitled 'My Own Stamp Album':

> Your Fascinating Folio of Philatelic Fun.
>
> Here's your magic key to a pastime that's taking the hobby world by storm—stamps! 'the calling cards of nations,' they've been termed. And we all know how fascinating it is to pore over a pile of old calling cards. And that's just a fraction of the fun, 'cause stamps are also educational! How else could you learn

> what it costs—in Turkish money—to airmail a letter from Turkey? Ready, set, grab your tweezers, and go![110]

Another of McCall's illustrated layouts is devoted to the 'Blessings of American Life' which includes Heated Shave Cream, Cheese Flavored Dogfood, Static Free Sox and Feminine Hygiene Sprays, but also stamp issues produced by Backward Nations, Somnolent Nations and Nations in Transition. We also learn that Great Britain was planning to issue a stamp to mark 'British Museum Opening Hours Extended' but that this was delayed due to a strike.

The humourist Beachcomber (a.k.a. J.B. Morton, 1893–1979) presented a somewhat original approach to stamp collecting. His creation, Lord Shortcake, was a fanatical collector of goldfish. But this was not all.

> In addition to collecting goldfish Lord Shortcake also collected stamps, but not foreign stamps, which, he said, should be left to foreigners. Instead he concentrated on British twopenny stamps. When people looking at his albums filled with twopenny stamps complained that they all looked the same, he would reply 'That is because you don't study them enough. All Chinamen look the same to many Westerners, but they really are all different.' Shortcake was quite indifferent to the correspondence he received. All that mattered was the twopenny stamp that might be on the envelope.[111]

A number of novelists and artists have sought to invoke the aid of postage stamps in order to find access to lost youth and the recent past. The famous semiotician and novelist Umberto Eco (1932–2016) had long been a collector of ephemera dating back to his boyhood in the 1940s—children's books, toys, film posters, Fascist propaganda—in the hope that these acquisitions would preserve his link with his past. He is best known for *Il nome della rosa* (1980; *The Name of the Rose*, 1983), an excellent novel featuring a medieval detective. He has also published numerous academic books on semiotics and aesthetics. But it is the not-so-excellent *La misteriosa fiamma della regina Loana* (2004; *The Mysterious Flame of Queen Loana*, 2005) which concerns us here. In this, his fifth novel, he conjures up Eco Yambo, an antiquarian bookdealer whose hobby is collecting literary references to fog. After suffering a stroke in his sixties, he wakes up in hospital having lost all his personal memories. He can remember books and references, but not his childhood, his friends or his former mistresses. He returns to the village of Solara and the old family home where he searches for objects which he once possessed or which meant something to him as a child in hope that such objects will somehow take him back to the youth he once was. There are frequent references to a children's story about Signor Pippino, who was born an old man but ends up dying as a bambino—surely some kind of metaphor for what is going on here. More generally, Yambo immerses himself in childhood memorabilia, of which the most colourful are comic books featuring Flash Gordon and other interplanetary or exotic adventurers.

(The novel is richly and enticingly illustrated with characters from comics, romances, postcards and stamps.) Though Queen Loana is the trashily conceived temptress of a romantic fiction whose story has been ripped off from Rider Haggard's adventure story *She*, Loana nevertheless continues to be the guardian of the mysterious flame of imagination that draws Yambo on in his quest for his childhood memories of adventure and first love. (It is a bit mysterious what is mysterious about the flame of Loana.)

Eventually Yambo comes across his stamp album which can be dated to 1943. He used to collect Italian stamps and at first he had amateurishly gummed the stamps to the pages of the album and later, no less amateurishly, tried to redress this by soaking them off the pages, but he eventually mastered the basics of philately. Though he has no memory of how the stamps were acquired, he can fantasise about their past significance:

> For me, that album must have been, more than a material object, a receptacle of oneiric images. I was seized with a burning fervour at the sight of each figure. Forget the old atlases. Looking through that album I imagined the clear blue seas, framed in purple of Deutsch-Ostafrika; I saw the houses of Baghdad, framed by a tangle of Arabian-carpet lines, against a night-green background; I admired a profile of George V, sovereign of the Bermudas, in a pink frame against a blue field; the face of the bearded pasha or sultan or rajah of Bijawar State—perhaps one of Salgari's Indian princes—subdued me with its shades of terracotta; certainly the little pea-green triangle from the Labuan

> Colony was rich in Salgarian echoes; perhaps I was reading about the war that started over Gdansk as I was handling the wine-coloured stamp marked *Danzig*; on the stamp of the state of Indore, I read FIVE RUPEES; I daydreamed about the strange pirogues outlined against in English.[112]

The stamps hint at a great childhood mystery, but it is one that he cannot quite recover. (The Salgari references, by the way, are to the former bestsellers of the prolific author Emilio Salgari (1862–1911), action-packed swashbuckling romances, many of which featured Sandoka, the Tiger of Malaysia, a prince of Borneo who has become a pirate and who fights against the British and Dutch hegemony in the East Indies.) There are two stamps that strike the narrator as intensely yet indefinably more significant than the rest. They are both Fijian issues. One shows a native and the other features a map of the islands. Wherein lay their fascination? Perhaps it was 'the map's precision, like a chart of treasure islands'? Perhaps.

It is clear that there is much that is autobiographical in *The Mysterious Flame of Queen Loana* and it draws heavily on Eco's Piedmontese childhood in the 1940s and 1950s. In an interview given in 2005 he revealed that for years he had been collecting the ephemera of youth. 'All during my adult life, every time I could in a flea market I re-set up my original library,' Eco says, adding that more recent searches helped him fill the gaps: 'Through the Internet I succeeded in reconstructing my stamp collection of 1945. More or less I have found exactly the same stamps I had in my collection . . . I have spent all my adult years continuously going back to my childhood.'[113]

It is time to return to those two mysterious Fijian stamps and their potent but ineffable significance. In the novel, Gragnola, an anarchist and former teacher, was an adult friend of the boy Yambo and after one conversation it emerges that Gragnola used to collect stamps, but later he lost interest and gave them all away except for twenty or so. These he was now prepared to give to Yambo, and this little gift includes the Fijian stamps that later stirred up so much longing for something forgotten on Yambo's part. These stamps now in his possession call up a memory of an evening with his mother and he is contemplating those stamps, which is when an allied plane flies overhead and woman on the radio sings: 'You'll come back, / because I / without all your languid kisses / won't survive'. Soon afterwards Gragnola, Yambo and a few others took part in a partisan operation to liberate some Ukrainians from their German captors. Yambo performed heroically, but Gragnola fell into the hands of the Germans. Rather than betray Yambo and others, he slit his throat with a lancet which he always had about his person in case he should be captured and tortured.

The exact significance of the two Fijian stamps remains undefined. It is likely that they remind Yambo of Gragnola and his sacrifice in the partisan war against the Germans. But that remains only an unspoken possibility. Why specifically the Fijian native and the map of the island? The principle of Anton Chekhov's gun should apply. According to Chekhov: 'If you say in the first act that there is a rifle hanging on the wall, in the second or third act it absolutely must go off. If it's not going to be fired, it shouldn't be hanging there.' But in Eco's novel, the protagonist scrutinises one example of childhood memorabilia and then another and then another, moving on and leaving the emotional or intellectual significance of each to dangle. As the narrative develops it seems that Yambo is on a quest to summon up in memory Lila, a girl at his school whom he adored, though he never dared declare his love for her (like Rostand's *Cyrano de Bergerac* perhaps). Lila is reported to have died young in Brazil. Yambo must seek to conjure in the magic theatre of memory the face of his first love. It is not clear if he succeeds, nor what success in this feat would mean. In the final, exceptionally densely illustrated chapter a romantic succession of heroes, heroines and villains parade down a broad staircase (that might have been borrowed from Powell and Pressburger's 1946 film *A Matter of Life and Death*), including Ming the Merciless, the Witch Queen Azura, Flash Gordon, Dale Arden, Mandrake the Magician, Sandoka, the Four Musketeers, Mickey Mouse and others. The parade is followed by a wilfully overwritten evocation of the glamour of his first love, only for this sort of fantasy to be rejected. 'No, no what wicked literature am I letting myself be seduced by, I am no longer a prurient adolescent . . . I would simply like her as she was, as I loved her then, just a face above a yellow jacket.' After this it may be that there is only death.

The Turkish novelist Orhan Pamuk (b.1952) made a more artful and convincing raid on his past. *The White Castle* (1985) was his first novel to attract widespread international attention. It was followed by *The Black Book* (1990), *New Life* (1994), *My Name Is Red* (1998), *Snow* (2002), *The Museum of Innocence* (2009), *A Strangeness in My Mind* (2014), among other novels. He was awarded the Nobel Prize for Literature in 2006. *The Museum of Innocence* is surely his masterpiece and it is a novel that does not suffer from being compared to *Madame Bovary* or *Anna Karenina* (and the reviewer in the *Financial Times* made exactly that comparison).

This novel, which verges on an encyclopaedia of lost love, nostalgia and everyday objects, is set in Istanbul primarily in the years 1975–80. Kemal, who is upper class, develops a passion for a shop girl, Füsun. She disappears when his engagement to another young woman is announced. Only then does he feel the full strength of his passion for Füsun, but by the time he tracks her down she is married. She is persuaded to allow him to make regular visits to the flat where she lives with her husband and parents. During those visits Kemal surreptitiously collects every object that he can which has been touched by her—cigarette stubs, empty lipstick holders, pillboxes, cinema tickets, postcards, matchsticks, old newspapers and so forth. During his eight years of visiting Füsun's flat, Kemal squirrels away 4,213 of her cigarette butts. He collects to mourn his loss. After her death in tragic circumstances, he turns her house into a Museum of Innocence in which those passionately accumulated scraps are displayed in a poignant evocation of lived experience.

Like Eco's novel, Pamuk's novel, at least in part, serves as a vehicle for the author to retrieve his own past. (He was in his early twenties in 1975.) In the novel and in Pamuk's life the cinema tickets, playbills, old newspapers and so forth are witnesses to the nostalgia Pamuk and Kemal feel for the material details of how Istanbul once was. Pamuk seemed possessed by fear of losing his memories of what 1970s Istanbul and its youthful inhabitants were like, and his fear mixed with nostalgia imposes a melancholy beauty on his city. The novel and an actual museum harbouring the ephemera of the past were planned in tandem, though it proved easier for Pamuk to complete and publish the book than to find premises suitable for the Museum of Innocence. The museum opened in 2012.

In *The Museum of Innocence* and in *The Innocence of Memories* (Pamuk's book about the making of a film about the actual Museum of Innocence) and in subsequent interviews Pamuk has offered many reflections on the nature of collecting and the psychology of collectors. From Kemal in the novel we learn:

> There are two types of collectors.
>
> 1. The Proud Ones, those pleased to show their collections to the world (they predominate in the West).
>
> 2. The Bashful Ones, who hide away all they have accumulated (an unmodern disposition).
>
> The Proud believe that what they have acquired should be destined for a museum, whereas the Bashful collect for the sake of collecting, and they keep quiet about it, because in the lands of the Bashful such collecting is the evidence of a psychological wound or inadequacy.[114]

In the mid-1990s Pamuk had begun collecting things for his future museum. He haunted flea markets, second-hand bookshops and dealers in ephemera and hunted in them for melancholy tokens of the past. In *The Innocence of Objects*, his account of setting up his own museum to explore the city of his youth, Pamuk suggested that pioneering collectors started their collections chiefly to establish a new identity for themselves.[115] In *The Innocence of Memories*, he noted that lots of everyday used objects just get thrown away: 'But there are a number of objects that fall into the category termed in the West as "collectables": matchboxes, lighters, bus passes, tickets to football matches, and, most importantly anything to do with old films.'[116] (Though Pamuk does not mention postage stamps, it is obvious that they must be ranked as both everyday objects and collectables.) In an interview Pamuk described a collector as 'a person who after a while cares about the possibilities of exhausting descriptions of that collection'. He also expressed a liking for collectors—and perhaps some pity. 'I think they are egoistic and slaves to the logic of their collections.'

ENOUGH OF NOVELS. Most novelists have not taken a particular interest in stamps and do not know much about them—and there is no reason why they should be so interested or knowledgeable. Exceptionally, Dennis Wheatley and David Benedictus did know about stamps, yet they did not produce better novels as a result. But here is another creative figure who made art from what yesterday discarded. The New York artist Joseph Cornell (1903–72) spent much of his life living in a small house with his mother and his disabled brother. Cornell was a somewhat reclusive figure who never travelled out of New York. He was a noted experimental filmmaker, but is probably best known today for his shadow boxes, that is boxes with glass fronts that are used to display objects. Cornell used to arrange mysteriously evocative assemblages of ephemera, effectively collages, in his shadow boxes. Such irrational assemblages of ordinary things delivered messages that were hard to decipher. They were like Surrealist paintings. He may have been the first American artist to become aware of what the European Surrealists were doing and he spoke of his admiration for the collages of Max Ernst and the paintings of René Magritte and, like the Surrealists, he accorded 'found objects' a special status. The Surrealists, for their part, admired Cornell's work and they welcomed his shadow boxes into their exhibitions. He haunted junk shops and flea markets questing for objects that were neither new nor antique, but which spoke of the recent past. (The German artist Kurt Schwitters occasionally used stamps in his collages to achieve a similar effect.) Cornell was in the business of collecting and packaging nostalgia. According to Susan Sontag, Cornell had 'the artist's temperament to an exquisite degree but he also had the temperament of a collector which is often not the same as an artist's temperament, in fact very often the collector is precisely someone who can't—who's fascinated by the beautiful but cannot create it, must collect it, but whose creative possibilities either don't exist or remain latent'.[117]

As a boy Cornell had collected stamps and as an adult he remained passionate about them, for they spoke to him about exotic places of which he dreamt but would never visit. Stamps were later included in a number of his boxes. For example postage stamps, including one Ottoman and one Chinese, feature in the box entitled *Habitat Group for a Shooting Gallery* (1943). Another to which Cornell gave no title, but which is known as *Music Box* (c.1947), was covered with a range of exotic stamps. Cornell remarked that the postage here was 'as if midway through an epic journey between a community of anonymous senders and recipients, never quite able to reach its elusive addressee'.[118]

In yet another box, untitled but known as *Penny Arcade* (c.1965), stamps contributed to an evocation of 'nostalgia for the enchantments of childhood'. Cornell's two hotel boxes, *Hôtel de la Duchesse-Anne* and *Hôtel du Nord*, make use of the same sets of stamps, butterfly stamps from Mozambique in 1953 and insect stamps from Portuguese Guinea 1953. The contents of these two boxes suggest that the hotels in question are exotic but tawdry. Stamps appear in yet another hotel box, *Ann—In Memory*. An inscription on the back of this box suggests that the stamps here from the Saar, Portuguese Mozambique and Haiti are part of a hotel box which commemorates a young prostitute who was briefly befriended by Thomas De Quincey. It is hard to see exactly how or why, yet it is true that the box does have a seedily romantic feel to it. Cornell gave 'cabinets of curiosity' a renewed meaning. They represented his nostalgia for travels and adventures that he had not actually experienced and never would.

My book has been compiled in the Autumn of Stamp Collecting. In J.B. Priestley's novel *Angel Pavement* one of its characters, a junior clerk, Stanley Poole, is practising to become a detective and the sort of person who shadows people without being spotted. A more senior clerk, a Mr Smeeth, asks him why he does not do something sensible in his spare time and take up a hobby:

> 'Do a bit of fretwork or collect foreign stamps or butterflies or something like that.'
>
> 'Huh! Nobody does them things now. Out of date,' Stanley muttered.[119]

Since Priestley's novel was set in the 1920s, that seems a decidedly premature verdict. Nevertheless there would come a time when it would be widely acknowledged that the heyday of stamp collecting was over. When British schoolboys in the nineteenth century and the opening decades of the twentieth opened their stamp albums, they were confronted by a treasury of images that affirmed and celebrated the stability and grandeur of the British Empire. Successive British colonial issues confirmed the continuing advance of the empire. In 1898, Canada, to celebrate the inauguration of the imperial penny postage, displayed the areas of the globe coloured pink together with the words 'We hold a vaster empire than has been'. But the popularity of stamp collecting was to decline *pari passu* with the shrinking of that empire after the Second World War and then the Suez debacle. There are still many in Britain who not only feel nostalgia for the disappearance of their empire but also for their childhood when they took pride in collecting its stamps. But by now stamp collecting has become very nearly as dated as bird's-nesting or collecting cigarette cards.

Robert Opie (b. 1947) was the son of the famous folklorists Iona and Peter Opie, the authors most notably of *The Lore and Language of Schoolchildren*. As a child Robert started as a stamp collector, but then switched to collecting other things that one could find in a Post Office. Finally he devoted himself to collecting food packaging and eventually established a museum of such boxes, tins and packets. The very commonness of such stuff, together with the transitory nature of their brands and designs, lends itself to nostalgia. In the museum such things speak powerfully of the 1950s. As Opie bears witness: 'If I haven't seen something for thirty or forty years it will give that intense "punch" of nostalgia, which happens to everybody.'[120]

Well, an empty tub of Trex may give rise to a brief pang caused by a sensation of how things were in the 1950s kitchen, but it is not likely to figure as a Proustian trigger to an entire lost world. According to Proust, 'Les vrais paradis sont les paradis qu'on a perdus.'[121] Susan Stewart has taken the deceitful matter further, since, as she sees it, the true object of (paradisal) nostalgia will not only have been lost, but it will never really have existed in the first place:

> Nostalgia is a sadness without an object, a sadness which creates a longing that of necessity is inauthentic because it does not take part in lived experience. Rather, it remains behind and before that experience. Nostalgia, like any form of narrative, is always ideological: the past it seeks has never existed except as narrative, and hence, always absent, that past continually threatens to reproduce itself as a felt lack.[122]

Personally, I find that nostalgia overlaps with false memory, since when I watch old documentaries about the 1930s and 1940s I often have powerful bouts of pseudo-nostalgia for the decades before I was born. In such spurious memories, it is as if, once upon a time, I have lived in a world of black and white, together with flappers, men in trilby hats and passing Cadillacs made like gleaming boxes on wheels. I cannot vouch for the accuracy of my presence at these scenes, but only for the anguished sense of what I dream that I have lost. But this is all digression.

THE HISTORIES of vanished territories, such as Kiautschou, Hejaz, Hatay, Heligoland and Corrientes, have pathos and in retrospect their stamps may function as nostalgia coupons. So often the issuing of a set of stamps was a feeble attempt at legitimation by regimes that were doomed to be short lived. But who knows? Things may change and times come round. (The London Library's obstinacy in retaining such apparently obsolete shelving categories as St Petersburg and Croatia was after many decades eventually rewarded.) Bjørn Berge collects representative stamps of every country or regime there has ever been. He prefers used stamps and he licks their backs to get their taste. To take one example, 'the taste is of crumbling gum arabic, vegetable starch and hide glue'. He takes note of the bitter ends of countries that no longer exist, but he is not entirely regretful: 'The motifs on the postage stamps give a fairly clear indication of what it's all about: an almost monolithic masculine culture of monarchs in all their pomp and circumstance, monuments to military conquest and loyalist heroes of all stripes (preferably represented as strutting peacocks or puffed-up chest-drumming gorillas).'[123]

If there are any real stamp collectors reading this, they must have winced to read of Berge's practice of licking his designated stamps. What is the point? Stamp collecting should not be confused with wine tasting. Even schoolboys know they should use stamp hinges. But not civil servants. Some years ago when I was researching the hajj in the Public Record Office in Kew I came across a file from an anxious official. Did King George V lick the backs of his stamps? Only, there was currently a typhoid outbreak spreading in Cairo's postal administration . . . (By the way, the king normally spent three afternoons a week on his stamps.)

Alan Bennett has a character in his play *The History Boys* remark that stamp collecting, like belief in God, is something that has passed away.[124] Nostalgia hurried close on the heels of the break-up of empires. It was not just the British Empire whose disappearance was registered in the catalogues of Stanley Gibbons and of Yvert et Tellier. 'The world of the stamp album was one of vanished and vanishing lands,' according to an essay by E.S. Turner. Turner, like Berge, brooded over so many territories that are unheard of outside the pages of the big stamp catalogues. He deplored the dreariness of renaming Van Diemen's Land as Tasmania. Moreover from 1918 onwards things became confusing: 'Stamps bearing portraits of Romanovs and Hohenzollerns were fast becoming curiosities. Many of the issues that mocked our indigence in shop windows bore the dramatic overprints of successful Allied Expeditionary Forces, or harsh black inscriptions like WAR TAX or WAR CHARITY, or the vengeful numerals 1918, or intimations of forthcoming plebiscites.' The territory of Fiume overproduced stamps. Wenden and Courland had become forgotten lands. As early as the 1980s approval sheets posted by stamp dealers for collectors to take their pick from were ceasing to be sent out.[125]

Nostalgia for the British Empire, other empires and other smaller and often stranger territories, some entirely imaginary, overlaps with other registers of nostalgia. As a boy I not only collected stamps and car numbers but also matchboxes, bubble-gum cards and cigarette cards. The material past was more present in the 1950s than it is now. For me the smell of Bakelite has a Proustian power to summon up my boyhood. Many of the books I bought and read as a child had been printed in the nineteenth century. Victorian pennies and half-pennies still circulated on the buses. (I still have my worthless collection of Victorian coppers.) More specifically the evidence of the Second World War survived its formal ending in the shape of bomb sites, prefabs, discarded gas masks, old ration coupons and amputee beggars. I bought sets of lead toy soldiers that typically included commandos with flame throwers and Germans with hands raised in surrender. The switch from lead soldiers to plastic ones only took place in the mid-1960s. Films like *In Which We Serve*, *Ice Cold in Alex*, *The Cruel Sea* and *The Dam Busters* presented dauntless British fighting men, but several of my schoolteachers had survived the war only to return to peacetime as broken men. I think that there were more American bases in England in the 1950s and early 1960s (and hence my collection of bubble-gum cards featured baseball players). There was much talk about the dimly sensed menace of Americanisation.

Toyshops were more common than nowadays and among other things they sold cap guns. Fireworks were sold by toyshops and newsagents. I wish I had collected firework casings, wrappings and boxes. They were so beautiful. Small stamp shops abounded. There used to be one on the concourse of Waterloo Station. There was another beside Guildford Station. There were also cinemas on the concourses of Waterloo and Victoria Stations. My brother and I were often left by our mother at a Guildford cinema so that she could go shopping. The children's matinee programme of short films, which was regularly preceded by an unappreciated organ performance, usually featured the ghastly Norman Wisdom and the wonderful Flash Gordon and Dale Arden. The Woking branch of Boots the chemist carried a circulating library which supplied me with the adventures of Tarzan.

Though England in the 1950s and early 1960s was in some respects rather dowdy, there was even so a kind of optimism and a fairground feel to the country. This was made manifest in the Festival of Britain in 1951. I remember the tree walk and the giant caterpillar roundabout in Battersea Park. *The Young Elizabethan* magazine provided regular instalments of stories and information about hobbies and sports together with optimistic and patriotic editorials. In my memory, the clouds over England were different in the 1950s and the skyscapes of films like Michael Powell's *A Canterbury Tale* and Humphrey Jennings's *A Diary for Timothy* tend to confirm my memory. The English countryside over which I roamed and where I still roam in retrospection was largely destroyed by the corrosive but necessary power of money. Looking back, it seems like an age of innocence, but, of course, the innocence was mine, not that of the age. Then came the 1960s. The *echt* 1960s, the 1960s of the beatniks, peaceniks, hippies and heads began around 1964 or 65 and I was part of that too and, to my shame, though the 1950s had nourished those of us who were to become hippies, we rated those years so little. As 'Going, Going', that wonderful poem of Philip Larkin, put it:

> I thought it would last my time
> . . . but all that remains
> For us will be concrete and tyres.

After Oxford, I decided to learn Arabic and do research on Middle Eastern history. Though I had several reasons for studying Arabic, including an abiding interest in the Crusades and an affiliation to Sufism, they were not the fundamental reasons for my wish to immerse myself in Arabic. I registered to do research at the University of London's School of Oriental and African Studies and there I met Patricia Crone (1945–2015), a Dane who, like me, was doing research on Middle Eastern history. She told me that she had decided to master Arabic as a way of exploring a language in order to see if mastery of a totally alien language would act as a portal to a completely different way of understanding the world and lived experience. This also had been my real underlying motive for choosing to study Arabic. In my first months of study, this seemed to be a good choice: the mismatch of the Arabic and European alphabets, the absence of capital letters, the changes in shapes of the letters depending on where they were in the word, the usual absence of short vowels (and in medieval Arabic also of punctuation), the gendering of verbs and the slapdash use of pronouns, all seemed to advertise the language's alien nature. (Patricia Crone, by the way, ended up as Professor at Princeton's

Institute for Advanced Study.) At first, my intuition about the alien nature of Arabic seemed correct, but within a year I was reading late medieval Arabic as if it was English. In retrospect the study of quantum physics and the origins of the universe would have been a much better bet for someone wishing to acquire a truly weird mindset.

When I moved from Oxford to London I fell on my feet. I found a lodging in Roupell Street, a well-preserved street of Georgian working-men's cottages. Its picturesque appearance led to its appearing in a number of feature films as well as an episode of *Doctor Who*. I paid one pound ten shillings a week for a room four times the size of a broom cupboard and which I shared with a hot-water boiler. The north end of the street was home to a network of young creative or academic people: a glass-blower and potter, a jewellery maker, a sculptor, an author and illustrator of a children's book, an anthropologist, an Egyptologist, a classicist. Retired circus people lodged further down the street. People popped in and out of houses and beds. As I got to know the people of the street and their farther-flung acquaintances, I began to collect coincidences and drew up a chart which recorded who knew whom, and which came to resemble a giant's cobweb. I have read that people who have a spiritual background are more likely to spot coincidences and thinking about coincidences brings them on. Also they tend to come in clusters. (Perhaps it has something to do with chaos theory.)

As for stamps, the market of Lower Marsh Street was only a short walk away and the stamp man had his pitch at the far end on Wednesdays, if I remember rightly. He always wore a trilby and a heavy overcoat. Most of his custom came from middle-aged businessmen who worked locally. He soon got to know that I was after stamps with Arabic lettering on them. The early issues of Middle Eastern stamps provided quite a training in reading Islamic calligraphy, since the shapes of the letters easily lend themselves to decorative distortion as letters may be elongated or set one above another or intertwined.

I used to be a would-be part-time hippy anarchist in those days, but in 1972 I got a job teaching medieval history in the University of St Andrews and within just a few years I had also acquired a wife, a daughter, a mortgage and a status of a sort. The transition was surprisingly easy. In 1977 I resigned from my university post and we returned to London and, as a house husband, I took over the day-to-day care of my one-and-a-half-year-old daughter. It was a fairly short walk from our house in Vauxhall over to Waterloo and Lower Marsh Street. Often on a Wednesday I used to put my daughter in the pushchair and, if she fell asleep on the way to Lower Marsh Street, as she often did, then I would stop pushing and I would take a notebook out of my pocket and make notes for a future novel. In Lower Marsh Street I re-established contact with the stamp man and my daughter was bribed with a Bounty bar not to distract us while I pored over what he had to offer. Despite that thick overcoat I heard that he died of pneumonia a year or two later.

It was all so long ago. In time stamp albums were liable to become portfolios of individual memories and nostalgia. In *Some*

Hobby Horses; or How to Collect Stamps, Coins, Seals, Crests and Scraps, C. Montrésor concludes:

> For, after all, the greatest delight which a collection of any kind can afford is the memory of the days in which it was formed; the happy holidays spent in 'arranging'; the bright birthdays, which added as a gift some longed for specimen; the little squabbles and arguments over doubtful treasures; the new ideas gleaned in 'reading it up'.[126]

A longing for something in the past that never truly existed is the purest form of nostalgia. Or, as Susan Stewart has put it, 'Nostalgia is sadness without an object', and, in her book *On Longing*, nostalgia is the thread that guides her in her study of 'narrative, exaggeration, scale and significance'. As we have seen, nostalgia suffuses the novels about collecting by Umberto Eco and Orhan Pamuk.

In the opening of *On Longing*, Stewart (b.1952) describes nostalgia as 'a social disease' (p.ix). She has already been quoted several times in what has gone before. She is a poet, critic, translator and Professor of English at Princeton. She published *On Longing* in 1984. This was a profound and subtle study of the way everyday objects are used in narratives to present particular versions of the world. Such thing-strewn narratives become structures of desire. She argues that miniature things become metaphors for interiority, and this kind of insight may earlier have had a role in Benjamin's enthusiasm for little things. It also seems likely that Stewart's musings on the miniature and interiority owe a great deal to Gaston Bachelard's *Poétique de l'espace* (*The Poetics of Space*) and so his reveries will be discussed below. Time ceases in the interior world of the miniature. In the contemplation of little things a flight from public to private becomes possible. (Though she does not mention postage stamps in the context of the miniature, obviously they qualify here.)

The souvenir is similar to a collected object, yet different from it: 'Like the collection, it always displays the romance of contraband, for its scandal is its removal from its "natural" location. Yet it is only by means of its material relation to that location that it acquires its value. In this is the tradition of "first-day covers" for stamps and the due disappointment we feel in receiving a postcard from the sender's home rather than the depicted site.' A souvenir is always metonymic, which is to say it is a part standing in for the whole (pp.135–6).

Although a collected object may at first embody memories in the collector of how, where and when it was spotted and acquired, in time this is likely to change: 'The collection replaces history with *classification* . . . all time is made simultaneous or synchronous within the collection's world' (p.151). So: 'We might therefore say, begging forgiveness, that the archetypal collection is Noah's Ark, a world which is representative yet which erases its context of origin' (p.152). (But note that Baudrillard, on whom see below, reckoned that Adam was the first collector.) Things like stamps, once they are placed in a collection, shed the context of their production. They lose whatever metonymic status they may have had.

ALLEGORICAL FEMALE FIGURES were much favoured by republican postal issuing authorities. In 1900 a new French definitive stamp was issued. It showed a seated woman in a Phrygian bonnet, laurel wreath and classical robe. She displayed a marble slab on which was written in capital letters 'Droits de l'homme' and she was supposed to be an allegory of the French Republic. In an article for the *Revue blanche* published on January 15, 1901, an eccentric writer described the image on the stamp as the likeness of a blind prostitute. (By the way, serious philatelists were also unimpressed by the stamp's design.) The eccentric critic of that French definitive issue seems to have had a broader prejudice against stamps:

> It is a superstition common among humans, who wish to converse with near relations from whom they are temporarily separated, for them to toss the written expression of their affection into some convenient orifice, such as the opening of a drain, after first having charitably encouraged the otherwise sinister trade in tobacco, by acquiring in exchange a few small images, doubtless blessed, which they then devoutly kiss on

> the backside; it is not our intention here to criticize the coherence of such practices, since it is undeniable that long-distance communication is made possible by their means.[127] (In France stamps are mostly sold by tobacconists.)

The anti-stamp writer in question was Alfred Jarry (1873–1907), the founder of Pataphysics, 'the science of imaginary solutions', a science, then, that is based on exceptions and accidents. Jarry was devoted to practical jokes and theatrical inventions, some of which involved Ubu Roi, a vulgar and vicious tyrant whose bizarre actions prepared the way for the Theatre of the Absurd.

In 1948 a Collège de 'Pataphysique was belatedly established to commemorate Jarry and to further pursue the science of imaginary solutions. Raymond Queneau and François Le Lionnais were the co-founders. Queneau was a well-known experimental poet, essayist and novelist. François Le Lionnais had trained as a chemical engineer and before the Second World War he had come to know various leading figures in Dada and in the overlapping world of chess. After the war, during which he had worked for the Resistance, had been tortured and sent to a concentration camp, he was employed as technical consultant for various high-ranking institutions. The diversity of specialisms and enthusiasms of Le Lionnais has been memorialised in a miscellany of writings entitled *Un certain disparate*. After outlining this much of the impressive career of Le Lionnais and exclaiming on his polymathy, Daniel Becker concludes as follows:

'He studied insulation problems in Parisian telephone lines, was a member of the Society for Basic Irreproducible Research and the Association Française des Artistes Prestidigitateurs . . . His last work, a compendium entitled *Nombres remarquables* (*Remarkable Numbers*), is dedicated to "my lifelong friends, delicious and terrifying, the numbers".'[128]

In 1960 Queneau and Le Lionnais went on to found the Ouvroir de littérature potentielle (Workshop for Potential Literature, commonly referred to as Oulipo). As has been noted in the discussion of Italo Calvino, this was a group who set out to explore possibilities offered by the use of mathematical and other constraints in fiction and poetry. Oulipo had emerged under the patronage of the Collège de 'Pataphysique. Its membership consisted of terrifyingly brilliant polymaths. Jacques Roubaud, Harry Mathews and Georges Perec were prominent members. Oulipians compared themselves to rats who had constructed the labyrinth from which they planned to escape.

Calvino called Georges Perec (1936–82) 'one of the most singular literary personalities in the world'. Perec's lipogrammatic novel *La Disparition* (1969; *A Void*) is a lengthy fictional tour de force in the course of which the letter 'e' is never used. His novel *La Vie mode d'emploi* (1978; *Life: A User's Manual*, 1987) offers stories based on the lives of the inhabitants of a Parisian apartment block. The protagonist Bartlebooth paints 500 watercolours of ports around the world, which, on his return to Paris, he turns into jigsaws and as each jigsaw is solved he destroys it, but he dies before he can accomplish this demanding though pointless feat. There are approximately 100 stories about the inhabitants of the apartment block and they are ordered according to a hidden formula. According to a review by Piers Burton-Page in *New Society*: 'Not the camera but the jigsaw is the *clef* to this *roman*. Such is its scope, such is the marvel of Perec's lapidary prose that the Chinese-box structure, the jokes and the typographic games enhance rather than diminish the vitality of those who people the puzzle.' In my review in *Time Out* I described it as 'one of the bizarre masterpieces of post-war fiction' and 'a revelation coming out of the blue, rich, bizarre and wonderfully entertaining'.

As a boy in Paris Perec had been a keen stamp collector. One day he ran away from home and headed for the open-air stamp market that was held in Carré Marigny, where he planned to sell his favourite stamps to help fund his flight. Though the stamp market was closed, as he had anticipated, he hoped that he might meet someone there to whom he might sell the stamps. He did not. After a long and hungry day travelling at random on the metro, a stranger took him to a police station and the police contacted his family. He wrote about the dismal adventure nearly twenty years later. Also he and a team of friends made a film in 1978, *Les Lieux d'une fugue*, which concentrated on places that had featured during his day as a boy on the run, including Carré Marigny and the metro.[129]

Life: A User's Manual is a fat book. In 1979 Perec published a very brief short story, *Le Voyage d'hiver* (*The Winter Journey*). This related how, shortly before the Second World War, a certain Vincent Degraël discovered a nineteenth-century book by an obscure writer, Hugo Vernier, entitled *Le Voyage d'hiver*, whose text contained many of the finest lines that were to be written by some of the most famous French poets who composed and published their verses in the years that followed the publication of *The Winter Journey*. Though this extraordinary phenomenon certainly needed to be investigated further, the Second World War intervenes and by the time Degraël can resume his mad inquiry into how this could be, the book has vanished and he will die in a psychiatric hospital.

Vernier's apparent achievement reminds one of the Surrealist concept of 'anticipatory plagiarism'. Though there is nothing in Perec's *The Winter Journey* to interest the philatelically minded, subsequently members of Oulipo added sequels to Perec's short story which had the effect of turning it into a hyper-novel, and the provisional text of this hyper-novel has been published in English as *Winter Journeys* (London, 2013). There are at least twenty-one of these Oulipian playful sequels. Paul Braffort's contribution 'Yvert's Journey', which was published in 2014, contains some philatelic references.[130] Paul Braffort (1923–2018) was an engineer, information technician, writer, poet and composer of songs. A friend of Queneau and Le Lionnais, he was not only a member of Oulipo but also an officer in the Collège de 'Pataphysique.

The title of Braffort's story alludes to Louis Yvert (1866–1950), the publisher of one of the first and most consulted French stamp catalogues which had been launched in 1895. But also, of course, Yvert and *hiver* are near homophones. The story starts with Braffort encountering Le Lionnais at a cybernetics conference in Namur and getting into a conversation with him about a book entitled *Mechanisms Common to Disparate Phenomena* (1921), published by Michel Petrovitch (1868–1943). Petrovitch was a Serbian mathematician, also a skilled fisherman and musician, and he did indeed publish (in French) the aforesaid phenomenological-cum-mathematical treatise. This is something I am incapable of shedding any light on and in any case it only serves as prelude to revealing that 'the little-known Society of Collectors of Triangular Stamps is among the many disparate societies that Le Lionnais belongs to'. I have been unable to confirm the existence of this 'little-known society'. Anyway, Braffort's account goes on to relate that Stanley Gibbons made his break as a stamp dealer by acquiring some Cape triangulars cheap and making a huge profit on them. Having asserted that the 'unusual and precious nature of these triangular stamps made their possession a natural subject for adventure stories and detective novels', Braffort compared them to the stamp in Ellery Queen's *The Chinese Orange Mystery*, 'in which the solution to the mystery lies in the decoding of an example of homophony'—a bit similar then to the linkage of 'hiver' to 'Yvert'. Braffort moves on to give an account of the career of Yvert. Two stamps in an Yvert et Tellier catalogue then become the focus of Braffort's attention: two portraits of logicians, first a Dutch stamp depicting Luitzen J. Brouwer (1881–1966) and secondly a Polish stamp showing a portrait of the wife of Leon Chwistek (1884–1944) painted by the multi-talented Polish logician and mathematician. Chwistek of course had disparate talents as he 'was also a novelist, playwright, graphic artist, painter, critic and philosopher as well as a logician'. Braffort's eventual meeting with Brouwer leads on to an account (which is completely incomprehensible to me) of a concept in mathematical logic known as the dichome and then the Principle of the Excluded Third (ditto).

Braffort's continuing 'philatelic-mathematical-literary researches' take him backwards and forwards across Europe and encompass logic, poetry, art, music and mysticism and require his attendance at disparate conferences. Numerous names of members of Oulipo feature as strained puns in Braffort's intellectually demanding Odyssey. His journey ends: 'And what better end could there be to this essay than a reproduction of a projected stamp which, not having been yet approved by the Post Office, appears in none of the *Yvert et Tellier* catalogues.' The projected stamp, which was illustrated in *Le Voyage d'hiver* and which unsurprisingly was never officially issued, is Stanley Chapman's 1965 design for an Oulipo/Pataphysical postage stamp which he modelled on Leonardo's *Last Supper*. Stanley Chapman (1925–2009) was an architect, designer, translator, writer, communist, Oulipian, Pataphysician and notorious grump.

THERE ARE PEOPLE who live fantasy rather than merely write it—among them the Kings of Redonda, Casanova, Aleister Crowley and Count Geoffrey Potocki de Montalk (the New Zealand-born King of Poland). Bruce Chalmers counts as another.

Bruce Condé (1913–92), whose original name was Bruce Chalmers, liked to be known as Abdurrahman Bruce Alfonso de Bourbon Condé. He was born in California and was adopted after being orphaned. As a child he was an avid collector of stamps. At one point he wrote to the Imam of Yemen asking him if he could let him have any stamps. The reply he got was from the Imam's stamp collecting young son, Muhammad al-Badr, and a friendship developed over the ensuing correspondence. During the Second World War Bruce served in North Africa as an intelligence major in the 82nd Airborne Division and picked up some Arabic, before being posted to Japan. After discharge from the army he went to Beirut where he resumed the study of Arabic. He also changed his surname to Condé, which had been his grandmother's surname, and this would furnish the preposterous pretext for his claim that he was descended from the French royal house of Bourbon Condé. Then he was invited by Muhammad al-Badr, now the Imam, to come to Yemen and there he renounced American citizenship, became a Yemeni and converted to Islam. After a time spent selling Yemeni stamps to collectors around the world, Condé persuaded the Imam to put him in charge of the Post Office where he could oversee the production of stamps destined to be sold to collectors. After a clash with the Minister of Communications, he was denounced as a spy, had his citizenship revoked and was expelled from the country in 1959. In Beirut he became a correspondent for an American stamp magazine. He was a particular expert on Japanese and Hawaiian stamps. Then he was invited to the emirate of Sharjah, one of the Trucial States which later became one of the United Arab Emirates. In Sharjah he established the tiny emirate's first Post Office and advised on the production of issues of stamps aimed at collectors. On one of the stamps he designed he expanded the frontiers of Sharjah, to the fury of Sharjah's neighbouring emirates.

In 1957 the Imam Yahya, ruler of what was at that time a united Yemen, started to open the medieval hinterland to Americans and Europeans. He also started to accept Soviet arms and advisers. That year *The Times* journalist David Holden arrived in the royalist capital of Taizz where he first encountered Condé whom he described as 'an American whose role was then obscure to me but who had materialised from the recesses of the guest house dressed in shoes, socks and a printed cotton kilt and was blessed, so he informed me, with the unlikely name of Bruce Alfonso de Bourbon Condé'.[131] As, in the course of his wanderings though the Yemen, he got to know Condé better, Holden characterised him as an ardent Yemenophile who tried to talk and dress like a Yemeni. He was 'an odd and slightly pathetic figure, somewhat out of his time and depth. Nervous, even in full flow he seemed to belong to nowhere and to be yearning romantically for the impossible.'[132]

In 1962 the death of the Imam and the succession of his son al-Badr sparked off a civil war between the Mutawakkilite Kingdom of Yemen and the Yemen Arab Republic, whereupon Condé returned to the kingdom and joined the royalist forces to fight against the republicans and their Egyptian supporters. In 1964 Condé became one of its generals and he also took over the production of royalist stamp issues (which had a vital fundraising role in the war). One set of stamps he issued showed a series of paintings from the Vatican whose themes suggested the essential unity of Christianity and Islam. In the wake of the royalists' defeat in 1970 he moved to Spain and later to Morocco. In both countries he supported himself by writing for stamp magazines. Stateless and impoverished in Morocco, he died of cancer in 1992. As for Muhammad al-Badr, after the royalist cause was abandoned by Saudi Arabia, he retired to England and is buried in Brookwood Cemetery.

Another adventurous character had a significant role in Arab stamp design. This was T.E. Lawrence, also known as Lawrence of Arabia. In 1916, as the First World War continued and Hussein, the Sharif of Mecca, had declared independence in the Hejaz, Lawrence and Ronald Storrs, Oriental Secretary of the Residency, were charged with selecting stamp designs for the newly formed kingdom of Hejaz. The chosen stamps would replace those of the Ottoman Empire and legitimise the new order in western Arabia. Enemy propagandists had been denying that the Arab Revolution was a success and 'we decided that the best proof that it had taken place would be provided by an issue of Hejaz postage stamps in Arabic, which could carry the Arab propaganda, self-paying and incontrovertible, to the four corners of the earth'.

The selected designs had to be non-figurative in order to suit the iconoclastic prejudices of so many of the inhabitants of the

Arabian Peninsula. So no portraits of the Sharif of Mecca, whom the British were backing as the ruler of this new sultanate, would be acceptable, and nor would images of dhows, riders on camels and other such markers of primitive exoticism. In the course of their wanderings around Cairo, Lawrence and Storrs selected a carved-stone pattern from the Saleh Tayyi Mosque, a stucco inscription from the entrance to the railway station and the elaborately decorated final page of a Quran in the Sultan Barquq Mosque. 'It was quickly apparent that Lawrence already possessed or had immediately assimilated a complete working technique of philatelic and three-colour production, so that he was able to supervise the issue from start to finish.'[133] Storrs was a notable aesthete and perhaps he minimised his own role in selecting and overseeing the design of the stamps. They were issued in 1916 and towards the end of that year Lawrence went out to the Hejaz where he would soon master the art of blowing up Turkish trains and participate in the capture of Aqaba.[134] Though the stamps were issued in 1916, it would be interesting to know when the Hejazi postal service really got going. In 1925 the Wahhabis of eastern Arabia invaded Hejaz, its Sharif fled and the Saudi leader Abdulaziz established the kingdom of Hejaz and Nejd (later to be redesignated Saudi Arabia).

IT IS TIME NOW to venture into the shadowlands of stamp collecting, a territory which is in large part populated by the comic, the preposterous, the inventive, the fraudulent, the inartistic, the indigent and the talentless. Cinderella stamps constitute a large part of the territory. According to L.N. and M. Williams: 'The group of Cinderellas is large. It includes local postage stamps, railway stamps, revenues, telegraph issues, phantoms and bogus stamps, Christmas seals, registration labels, and several other classes; in fact it embraces most of those categories which catalogue publishers have shunned.'[135] Alternatively a Cinderella stamp can be defined as anything resembling a postage stamp but not used for postal purposes by a government issuing body.

In Robert Graves's novel *Antigua, Penny, Puce*, a clergyman standing beside Oliver at a stamp auction declaims against a 'new fashion in philately', Cinderella stamps:

> 'Official air-mail stamps by all means. Duly accredited, I mean. Must move with the times. But cachets and covers, no! semi-official issues, still less. No right to be offered in these rooms. Look here! "First aerial delivery, 1913. Robert Sinclair Tobacco Company, Sinclair vignette. Block of ten, mint." Can't call those *stamps*. Might as well take the bands off cigars and call them stamps.'

Among the Cinderellas, Felter has distinguished between the phantom and the bogus. Phantom stamps are issued by imaginary countries that do not otherwise exist, whereas bogus stamps come from real countries, but those countries have not issued the stamps in question.[136] For example, in 1919, in the wake of disorders attendant on the outbreak of the Russian Revolution two years earlier, the short-lived Azerbaijan Democratic Republic issued Azerbaijan's first stamps, before being occupied by the Red Army. Subsequently the Azerbaijan Soviet Socialist Republic sporadically issued sets of stamps, but the 1923 Azerbaijani famine relief pictorial set was wholly bogus and was probably printed in Italy. Similarly the Odessa famine relief charity stamps of 1922 were never used in Russia, but were faked in Italy. By the way, the designs of those stamps were rather stylish.[137] Such stamps were usually produced in western Europe in order to be sold to collectors. But the alleged 1999 Abkhazian stamp depicting Bill Clinton in underpants with Monica Lewinsky must have had a more mischievous intention.

Then there are stamps that come from territories which never existed as stamp-issuing states. For example, Oecussi-Ambeno exists as a regional enclave of the island of Timor, but it has never been a genuine state. It was brought into a shadow existence in 1968 by the New Zealand artist Bruce Grenville and some of his anarchist friends. (As has already been mentioned, Grenville later worked to create the philatelic output of Fantipo.) Though Oecussi-Ambeno could be found in an atlas, the fact that almost nobody had even heard of it gave free rein to Grenville's imagination and during the 1970s and 1980s he decided to be its sultan. Grenville has pointed out that the production of stamps for imaginary countries is not necessarily a simple matter, since in order for the stamps to be 'right', the issuing country behind those stamps must be thoroughly imagined. So one must work on the non-existent regime's head of state, its national emblem and its history, as well as the local postmarks. Grenville also worked on the entire history from 1848 of the Sultanate of Oecussi-Ambeno and he sought diplomatic relations with Monaco and Liechtenstein. Soon after word of the Sultanate spread, a deluded international consortium came together to fund some of the earliest colourful issue of its stamps.[138]

The Sultanate of Upper Yafa, which had indeed a brief existence in a mountainous region in the north of Yemen, survived as an ally of the British Aden Protectorate. The village of Mahjaba with its mud-brick towers was its capital. When the People's Republic of South Yemen, a communist regime, was established in 1967, Upper Yafa was absorbed into it. Nevertheless that was the year stamps of Upper Yafa briefly appeared on the market. Though the stamps were officially authorised, they were exclusively aimed at collectors and were thematic 'collectables' that featured the Olympic Games, the works of Leonardo, the World Cup, the assassination of Kennedy, dancers painted by Degas and so forth. The stamps were printed in London. There was no Post Office in Upper Yafa.[139] Then, in the 1970s and 1980s the New Zealand anarchist Bruce Grenville (him again) resurrected Upper Yafa with a series of distinguished-looking stamps which made use of both English and Arabic scripts. In what appears to be the culminating issue, 'Upper Yafa honours God with new stamps'. The soi-disant Minister of Posts issued the following communiqué: 'Rather than force our postal patrons to adorn their letters with stamps marking the centenary of this or the fauna of that, our Post Office is issuing what we believe is the ultimate commemorative: an attractive and dignified set honouring God, the Creator of the universe, the compassionate, the merciful.'[140]

Adanaland is unusual in being an imaginary territory that is situated in West London. It has produced a range of thoroughly respectable-looking stamps. According to its handbill:

> The Kingdom of Adanaland is a time-warped enclave to the West of London, which may be glimpsed in the pages of old catalogues of the Adana printing machine company. Its population is composed largely of self-employed tradesmen who, in their leisure hours, enjoy tea dances, whist drives, masonic meetings and healthy outdoor sports.
>
> Adanaland has a number of overseas colonies and maintains friendly diplomatic relations with other oneirophilatelic states throughout the world. Its stamps are produced at the Hedgehog Press in Wivenhoe. (pp.18–21)

By the way, useful information about the necessary procedures for issuing postage stamps, passports and flags and choosing a national emblem is obtainable from *How to Start Your Own Country*, by Erwin S. Strauss.[141]

Redonda has the doubtful merit of really existing.[142] It is a small Caribbean island, close to Antigua and Montserrat, and is about one mile long, with no source of freshwater except rainfall, and it is almost always uninhabited. Matthew Phipps Shiel was born on the island of Montserrat in 1865. His father, Matthew Dowdy Shiell (sic), claimed sovereignty over Redonda before the British had got around to doing so. It is alleged that Shiell had purchased the island, but as Javier Marías has pointed out, no one knows exactly from whom, as the only inhabitants at the time were the boobies who populated it, alongside a handful of men who spent their time collecting the birds' excrement in order to make guano. Then it is alleged that when his son was fifteen he took him to Redonda and had him crowned King of Redonda in the presence of a Caribbean clergyman.

Subsequently Shiel, who took the title of Felipe I, was to preside over Redondan affairs from various flats and pubs in London, especially in the district of Fitzrovia. He was a remarkably prolific author of fictions written in a no less remarkably decadent mannered prose. Though a lot of his oeuvre is unreadable today, some of his weird science fiction and mystery novels gets regularly reprinted, most notably *The Purple Cloud* (1901), in which a polar explorer seeks to return to civilisation from the North Pole only to discover that civilisation has been destroyed in his absence. Shiel died in 1947.

Prior to Shiel's death he passed the kingdom on to John Gawsworth (1912–1970), his literary executor and drinking companion, who assumed the regnal title Juan I. Gawsworth, a writer, poet and anthologist, was probably better known as a habitué of pubs than as a writer. (By the way, Gawsworth was not his real name, which was Terence Ian Fytton Armstrong. Why, I ask myself, would anyone who has gone to the trouble to change his name change it to Gawsworth.) He was a great admirer of the writings of Shiel and of the horror writer Arthur Machen. Shiel had made little of his shadowy claim to kingship and referred to it belatedly, occasionally and elliptically. Gawsworth took the business of being royal more earnestly. He admired his friend Machen so much that he made him the sole archduke among the newly created peerage of Redonda. Other writers who were honoured with peerages included Gerald Durrell, Lawrence Durrell, John Heath-Stubbs, Henry Miller, Stephen Potter, J.B. Priestley, Arthur Ransome, Dorothy L. Sayers, Dylan Thomas, Rebecca West and Ellery Queen. As readers who have come so far with this book may have surmised, there is perhaps something problematic in the award of a dukedom to the trinity that constituted Ellery Queen.

Though much of the list of dukes of Redonda was impressive, it seems that others may have achieved ennoblement by buying Gawsworth drinks. The Redondan court often met in the Fitzroy Tavern, a pub a little way north of Soho. Lawrence Durrell wrote a short memoir in which the alcoholic decline of the writer-king was movingly recorded. Later Gawsworth featured in Javier Marías's novel *Todas las almas* (1989; *All Souls*, 1992). The writer and publisher Jon Wynne-Tyson wrote on the occasion of Gawsworth's death:

> The legend of Redonda is and should remain a pleasing and eccentric fairy tale; a piece of literary mythology to be taken

> with romantic sighs, appropriate perplexity, some amusement, but without great seriousness. It is, after all, a fantasy that has already passed into history and even into some history books; a fact which qualifies it to be seen as both bunk and as inspiration.

As Marías was to observe, Redonda was an island 'inherited through irony and writing'. In 1970, the year of Gawsworth's death in hospital, he passed the Kingdom of Redonda on to Wynne-Tyson, who was also made his literary executor, and Wynne-Tyson thereupon took the title Juan II. In 1979 Wynne-Tyson and a small band of Redonda enthusiasts made a somewhat perilous landing on the coast of Redonda, which they thought was uninhabited. Almost. Amazingly the first thing they encountered was a functioning Post Office where its part-time postmaster was able to serve them stamps. These must have been the 1979 issue of Antiguan stamps overprinted 'REDONDA'. The Post Office had just been set up and the stamps overprinted by Antigua in advance of Antigua's and Montserrat's independence from Britain in order to strengthen their claim to Redonda. At that time the postmaster was the island's only inhabitant. His tenure of this not very demanding job does not seem to have lasted very long and today only a few foundation stones of the Post Office remain visible.

From the first, Wynne-Tyson's succession to the throne had been disputed, and by the 1990s there were at least a dozen rival claimants and he was finding it increasingly time-consuming having to defend himself from their attacks and dealing with other Redondan business. In 1997 he abdicated in favour of the famous Spanish novelist Javier Marías (1951–2022), who took the title Xavier I. Marías was born in Madrid in 1951. He had an international reputation as a novelist, translator and academic and won many awards. Like De Quincey, Proust and Ciaran Carson, Marías favoured lengthy sentences, digressions and a rather formal manner of exposition. The paragraphs coil down the pages like snakes. As noted, Gawsworth featured in his novel *All Souls* which draws on Marías's time as an academic from 1983 to 1985 in Oxford.[143] For much of its length *All Souls* (which is the name of an Oxford college) reads like a series of loosely linked short stories and essays which tend to begin with concrete observations before moving on to abstract reflections. The book's underlying unity only becomes evident towards its end. The impression that *All Souls* made on Wynne-Tyson had led him to pass on the crown to Marías.

There are a number of factual errors in the narrative of *All Souls* which are so egregious that they are likely to be deliberate. For example, when reminiscing about his acquisition of the seventeen volumes of Richard Burton's *The Thousand Nights and a Night*, the unnamed narrator of *All Souls* declares that it was printed 'in a limited edition of a thousand numbered copies of each volume, available only to subscribers of the Burton Club on the understanding (which they honoured) that it would never be enlarged or reprinted: in fact that exuberant Victorian text has never again been reprinted in its entirety, but only in selections or in bowdlerised editions, which, whilst apparently complete, were in fact expurgated of everything considered at the time (or by Lady Burton) to be obscene'. This is not correct. The ten volumes were published in 1885 and the six supplementary volumes (later split into seven) were only produced in 1886–8. I have on my shelves a complete set of what appears the first edition of the first ten volumes together with a set of the seven supplementary volumes. None of Burton's stories has been omitted or bowdlerised in these volumes. Again, regarding the 1937 survey *Authors Take Sides on the Spanish War*, it is claimed by Marías that the horror-story writer Arthur Machen was the only writer to declare for Franco. In fact, Evelyn Waugh, Edmund Blunden and two other authors of lesser renown did the same.

So what was going on? Perhaps the author-cum-narrator was teasing or testing the reader. Perhaps the aim was to heighten the wickedness of the horror writer and perhaps also to exaggerate the rarity of the discriminating book purchase by Marías. Perhaps he simply did not care about getting things right. Perhaps he was being kind and wanted observant and pedantic readers to feel good about themselves. But in *Dark Back of Time* (a later novel, on which see below), in a passage devoted to the revelation of the apparent identity of the narrator of *All Souls*, he made the following confession in another context:

> It wasn't a mistake or an oversight, a thoughtless intrusion or moment of forgetfulness, it was deliberate, for, as I said before, these are the most autobiographical pages in the novel and it seemed honourable to tacitly confess that by means of this

> apparent slip which, as was to be hoped and expected, passed unnoticed by those who read it. (I also did it for the risk, one is always tempted to throw in some blots and smudges, for love of transgression and to betray oneself, and to see if they can pass for unblemished text.)[144]

As monarch, Marías inherited the acrimonious correspondence that Wynne-Tyson had found such a burden, but he declined to enter into arguments about the matter. He was also discriminating in his bestowal of peerages to such cultural grandees as the writers A.S. Byatt, Orhan Pamuk, W.G. Sebald, Umberto Eco and the filmmaker Pedro Almodóvar. In 2000 the succession dispute grew heated when Marías was accused of being an impostor or usurper. A certain John Robert claimed that he ruled Redonda as Juan II, since he had purchased the kingdom from his friend Gawsworth in 1967. During his contested tenure Robert tried to make the kingdom respectable. In 1989 his wife's illness led him to abdicate and pass on the throne to William Leonard Gates, who assumed the title Leo I. Marías did not directly engage with his rival but discussed his own succession to the kingdom in his later novel *Negra espalda del tiempo* (1998; *Dark Back of Time*). This novel, whose title derives from a modified quotation of Prospero in *The Tempest*, is in part a continuation of *All Souls* and a commentary on it. In the first half of *Dark Back of Time* Marías mounts a playful defence of *All Souls* from accusations that it was just a *roman à clef* which drew on his two years teaching Spanish in Oxford, the eccentric dons he knew there and the adulterous affair he enjoyed with one of the teachers, yet he (deliberately) protests too much and casts further doubts on the relationship between truth and fiction in this novel and life in general. Most of the second half of the book is devoted to the thoroughly obscure careers of minor literary figures. The two halves are intricately cross-referenced. Each man's death is presented as his destiny. Only in the final twenty pages or so of the book, which is over 300 pages long, does he give an elliptical account of Redonda and how he became its king. Perhaps he planned a sequel. He welcomed his kingship as an obligation that he had taken on by virtue of his destiny as a writer. 'I shouldn't be termed a real novelist if I didn't accept the novelesque in my own life when it came.' The dark back of time is to be understood as both forgetfulness and death. He died of complications attendant on Covid on September 11, 2022, aged seventy.

SO FAR THIS BRIEF ACCOUNT of the establishment of the Kingdom of Redonda, the succession of kings after Felipe I and the disputed lines of succession after the abdication of Juan I has been of little or no apparent relevance to what appears to be the subject of this book, since none of the so-called heirs to the Kingdom of Redonda authorised the issue of postage stamps. Instead, the immediately foregoing discussion has been by way of digression. Such interruptions are usually agreeable. As Lawrence Sterne observed in *Tristram Shandy*, 'Digressions, incontestably, are the sunshine;—they are the life, the soul of reading;—take them out of this book for instance,—you might as well take the book along with them.' In his novel *The Life and Opinions of Tristram Shandy* (nine volumes, 1761–7), the proliferation of digressions means that Tristram, who narrates, does not get to his birth until volume three. Yet Tristram maintained that 'I progress as I digress'. The philosopher John Locke's *An Essay Concerning Human Understanding* (1689), with its theory of the association of ideas, seems to have furnished the guiding principle for Tristram's manner of narrating. At the age of twenty-five Marías translated *Tristam Shandy* into Spanish and he later claimed that this labour made him into a novelist. The translation took him two years, in the course of which he said that he had learned that anything may go into a novel. Locke had argued that two or more ideas of things customarily became associated with one another not by logic, but by nearness in time, or physical proximity or habit. By the way, Locke's way of thinking about thought and sensation also influenced De Quincey's formulation of the involute. Early on in his *Dark Back of Time* Marías described it as 'a book of digressions, a book that proceeds by digression'. Literary digression by its nature has many purposes. Playful twists and turns of a narrative may serve as a deliberate technique for building narrative tension, as the reader impatiently asks when will this digressive writer get to the bloody point. On the other hand, it may be that the digressive author is actually afraid of his reader. He is afraid of being boring and so he switches from subject to subject. He does not know how his main argument should run and what his conclusion should be, so he thinks of something else to write first and then something else . . . He does not know how it will end, but he fears that it will end badly. But in the medieval Arab lands, digression took a more confident form with the alternating deployment of *hazl* (joking) with *jidd* (seriousness). The difficulties inherent in a demanding topic might be alleviated by one or more playful digressions, though literary convention required that the alternation of *hazl* and *jidd* should always terminate with *jidd*. The ninth-century Basran essayist al-Jahiz was the pioneer and master of this literary technique, and 'Lest I tire the reader' is a common phrase in his prolific writings. Centuries in advance of Locke, al-Jahiz allowed the association of ideas rather than strict logic to determine the course of his arguments.

Then, of course, the senile or those advancing towards senility are peculiarly prone to digression as they lose one thread of narration or argument after another. Though this is no kind of rhetoric and its victims must be accounted to be involuntary practitioners of digression, there are nevertheless relatively youthful imitators of the old who consciously deploy artificial digressions in order to simulate the hesitant voice of an aged narrator and hint at the failings, or it may be the eloquence, of the passing of the years.

Yet textual digressions may have a more mysterious purpose. They may question the workings of coincidence and suggest the interconnectedness of all things; for example De Quincey's early admiration for Rowland Hill while that man was still teaching at Bruce Castle, Tottenham, and had not yet got round to inventing the postage stamp. Then there is the influence of *Tristram Shandy* on Javier Marías, and it was Marías who wrote in *Dark Back of Time* 'of that bearable, brief fear that comes over us when we see things unexpectedly and with too much precision, the fear that the world is more orderly than we like to believe, or that we are better at ordering it'. Certainly there is more to life than logically sequential thinking. Does not our thinking normally take the form of a series of digressions, moving on from perhaps reflections on *War and Peace* to wondering what there is for breakfast and from there to admiring the play of sunshine on a puddle? In this fashion the whole of life is a kind of reverie.

Digression takes one back to De Quincey and his literary style which was shaped by sentences of serpentine length and structure, as well as by afterthoughts, corrections, digressions and opium. When he described his frequent nocturnal rambles through the streets of London, it is also his manner of writing that is on his mind: 'And sometimes in my attempts to steer homewards, on nautical principles by fixing my eye upon the pole-star, and seeking ambitiously for a north-west passage, instead of circumnavigating all the capes and headlands I had doubled in my outward voyage, I came suddenly upon such knotty problems of alleys, such enigmatic entries, such sphinx's riddles of streets, without thoroughfares, as must, I conceive, baffle the audacity of porters and confound the intellects of hackney coachmen.'[145]

Indeed this last paragraph has been a digression founded upon a digression.

RELUCTANTLY I NOW RETURN to the subject of stamps and their collection and, more specifically, the stamps of Redonda. While it is true that none of the Kings of Redonda commissioned the issue of stamps (as far as I know), nevertheless, as already mentioned, in 1979 a set of Antiguan stamps which featured Queen Elizabeth's head were formally put on the market overprinted 'REDONDA' and these Antiguan stamps were what the lonely postmaster would have sold to his visitors. Shortly thereafter more ambitious varied sets of alleged Redondan stamps appeared. They commemorated the Rotary International; the work of Picasso; the wedding of Charles and Diana; the Spanish World Cup; Disney's *One Hundred and One Dalmatians*; seventy-five years of scouting and so on. The latest that I have seen date from 1991. These issues were produced by London-based printers who often printed stamps for legitimate stamp-issuing countries, but they also put out stamps that had no authentic postal authority. One of these firms, Format International Security Printers Ltd, who printed Redondan stamps from 1976 to 1987, has a website which promises that 'Collector stamps are fun!' Other stamp-producing firms have also been involved in producing this sort of thing, and, such is the barmy world of stamp collecting, there are collectors who specialise in this kind of stamp. Such stamps count as 'collectable'.

We come now to the outright badlands of stamp collecting. Whatever the old guard of philatelic purists (and I am with them) may think of such collectables as issues devoted to Disney films or royal weddings, at least the themes are cheerful. The Iranian authorities are not so obsessed with bringing smiles to happy faces of the users of its stamps. Commonly they depict scenes of carnage, successful terrorism, imperialist outrages which must be avenged and glorious but bloody military triumphs. Such images would commonly require wall posters to achieve their desired propagandist effect and it is a little odd to see such atrocities miniaturised. But the most commanding image is that of the turbaned and unsmiling Ayatollah Khomeini. Though, by the way, the folklore that the Ayatollah never smiled is untrue, for there are plenty of photographs of him smiling and certainly it must be conceded that the display of a grinning Ayatollah would be inappropriate on the stamps issued by the government of a country which has suffered so much from the bloody aggression of the Iraqis, Israelis and Americans and which has done so much to retaliate. And, come to think of it, the Queen on the Penny Black was not smiling either.

A forged stamp should be regarded as a special kind of Cinderella stamp, but in practice it is usually discussed separately. If you must become a philatelist, then I sigh for you. Among other things, you will have to master the specialised vocabulary that goes with the hobby and it will be no good relying on the woolly definitions provided by the standard dictionaries of the English language. Consider the example of the respective philatelic meanings of 'counterfeit', 'forgery' and 'fake'. A counterfeit is a stamp which has been created with the intention of defrauding the postal authorities. They are quite rare. A forgery has been created with the intention of fooling the collector. A fake is a real stamp that has been tampered with in order to make it seem rarer than it is. There is more than one way of making money from forgeries. A certain François Fournier in Switzerland produced fake stamps, allegedly as a service to collectors who could not afford the real rarities. These stamps were marketed as replicas. But of course, despite the seeming innocence and legality of Fournier's advertised intentions, it would always be possible for his less scrupulous customers to sell on their purchases as if they were genuine.[146] Fournier claimed to see his creations as facsimiles or art objects. He also presided over the repair of damaged stamps and the 'repair' might involve removing the postmark. Then again some forgeries are worth more than the genuine stamps they were based on. It follows from this that there are also known cases of fake forgeries. There are also forgeries of bogus stamps such as the Azerbaijani famine relief stamps which were never really issued but were later forged. There are no special words for these categories of stamp, though there are several handbooks on them. And beyond this, it may be that there are forged fake forgeries??? Yet E.S. Turner had a good word to say about postal forgeries: 'This criminal taint gave a pleasing edge to the hobby; nobody, as far as we knew, had ever bothered to forge cigarette cards.'

The forging of stamps has not been restricted to small gangs or individuals. Sometimes governments took a hand. During the Second World War Britain's Office of Strategic Services forged stamps somewhat resembling the definitive issue featuring Hitler's head, except that beneath the familiar features of the Führer his skull could clearly be seen breaking through his skin and the words *Futsches Reich* (Ruined Empire) appeared beneath the head. These stamps were attached to plausibly addressed envelopes, bagged up and then dropped by bombers over Germany. This was known as Operation Cornflakes. In another piece of skulduggery the British issued another series of stamps somewhat resembling the Hitler's head on the definitive series, but with Himmler's head substituted. This was distributed among various countries with the aim of spreading the rumour that a coup had taken place in Germany. Germans, for their part, issued fakes of British stamps in which the inserted hammers and sickles and the Stars of David suggested that Britain and its monarch were the tools of Stalin and the Jews.

Naturally much of the philatelic propaganda was aimed by wartime regimes at their own citizens. To take a particularly egregious example, in 1942 the Serbs issued a set of stamps to commemorate the antisemitic exhibition that had opened in Belgrade in the previous year. The stamps, which drew heavily on the antisemitic *Protocols of the Elders of Zion*, also targeted the Freemasons. The forces of light glowed strongly behind muscular Serbs ('free', but part of the Nazi empire) in combat with the forces of darkness. Since the images were allegoric, they gave no guidance as to what exactly the Jews and Masons were doing in their darkness. After the war all sorts of countries, such as St Lucia and St Kitts, which were set on targeting the collectables market, issued stamps with Masonic imagery which were entirely benign.

But we have strayed from forgeries as a means of generating income. There are other illegitimate ways of making money out of stamps. Howard Marks (1945–2016) was to acquire recognition as a writer and notoriety as a dealer. He was at Balliol College, Oxford, from 1964 to 1967. While an undergraduate he only traded in cannabis, but later in London he became a partner in dealing in hashish from Pakistan and Afghanistan. The problem soon arose with the police and other authorities of how to explain all the money he was making. Two solutions were eventually adopted. First, he set up a smart dress shop called Annabelinda on Gloucester Green, Oxford. Secondly, he drew on his philatelic expertise:

> Another office was set aside to convert my hobby of collecting stamps into a philatelic business. My plan was to buy in my own name massive quantities of unsorted stamps, known in the trade as kiloware, at cheap prices. At the same time, expensive rare

> stamps would be bought anonymously by me for cash from reputable dealers in the Strand. My business records would state that these valuable stamps had been recovered from the kiloware after a painstaking, time-consuming search. I would then sell the valuable stamps to stamp dealers in the provinces and appear to be shrewdly making legitimate money. There would be some financial loss, but who cared?

He claimed to be a dealer specialising in 1922 overprints. (It is just possible that Marks may have got the idea of pretending to go through big, unsorted packets of stamps, scrutinising them carefully in search of errors and other rarities, from Simenon's novel *The Little Man from Archangel* in which a stamp dealer was presented as genuinely discovering rare stamps in big unsorted packets and so going on to establish himself as a leading figure in the philatelic trade.) Marks's career as drug and stamp dealer appears to have come to an end when he was arrested in the United States and sentenced to twenty-five years. He was released in 1995 after seven years and died in 2016. His autobiography, *Mr Nice*, was published in 1996. A biography, *High Time: The Life and Times of Howard Marks*, was published in 1984.

Apart from forgeries, among the many other kinds of postage stamp which are not recognised as having any legal validity, Artistamps form a large category. Despite their name, such stamps only occasionally have much aesthetic merit. (The oeuvre of Donald Evans with its superb miniatures of Dutch landscapes and exotic fruits is a rare exception here.) Producers of Artistamps often subscribe to anti-authoritarian impulses. Some protest against the postal monopolies of governments. Others silently demonstrate against authoritarian or banal images on officially authorised stamps. Yet others aim at miniaturised pornography. It may be needless to remark that these are unthreatening protests. The 'Fifth World' of independently produced stamps whose images delight or horrify the eye have covered such unusual topics as naked sporting events, Moscow manhole covers, life in a concentration camp, stallions mounting mares, extra-terrestrials, Kurt Schwitters, high heels, bananas, the Year of Tibet, crosswords, whale as a source of nutrition, Carlos the Jackal and boobs.

In avant-garde Chicago two artists, Michael Thompson and Michael Hernandez de Luna, produced their own stamps for use in the mail. When they were threatened with prosecution by the United States Postal Inspection Service for using fake stamps for postage, they denied that they were criminals: 'We're pranksters, we're punks.'[147] James Warren Felter, another Artistamp man, has provided a comprehensive guide to the little-known Artistamp miniaturised world of imaginary islands, obscene acts, virtual countries and parodies of officialdom, together with brief profiles of Hernandez de Luna, Donald Evans, Bruce Grenville and others.

The Mail Art Movement, which involves artists circulating their work to each other via the postal system in a so-called network, aims as Guy Bleus states, to 'democratise, decentralise and dematerialise artistic production'. Bleus is perhaps best known for his creation of interplanetary stamps for the inhabitants of Mars and visitors from Earth. (While on interplanetary matters, a fair number of stamps have been issued in recent decades commemorating visitations of flying saucers by, among others, Madagascar, Mali and Kazakhstan.)[148]

Thousands of artists participated in Fluxus, Mail Art, the Artistamp movement and similar groups. Only a few representative figures will be highlighted in what follows. Fluxus, which flourished in the late 1950s, 1960s and 1970s, was a very loosely associated international group of experimental artists and designers who placed their emphasis on the process of creating rather than on the finished product. They were against commercialism and what they created was often playful. Robert M. Watts (1923–88) was a Professor of Art at Rutgers University, but better known as one of the founding figures of Fluxus. He initiated festivals and all sorts of stunts, as well as working with found objects and other things. Although he was well known in the Artistamp world, only a small part of his work was philatelic. He sometimes substituted his stamps for those of the postal service, which nevertheless was kind enough to deliver them. Watts also invented the 'Postman's Choice' card and stamp for which the postman decides the destination. Some of the stamps he designed had erotic themes.

James Francis Cauty, also known as the musician Rockman Rock, was born in 1956. A guitarist, he played with rock groups before forming a partnership with Bill Drummond. Albums were issued and they played around with various pop anarchist ideas. In 1993 Cauty burnt £1 million on the island of Jura and a screening tour of this financial sacrilege followed. In 2003, after the British government had alleged that Saddam Hussein possessed weapons of mass destruction, Cauty had an exhibition in Brighton which, among other controversial items, featured stamps of Queen Elizabeth II wearing a gas mask. These were identified as first-class, second-class and third-class Stamps of Mass Destruction. The Royal Mail threatened prosecution. Nevertheless, fourth-, fifth- and sixth-class Stamps of Mass Destruction followed in 2004. After all that Cauty's stamps were seized and destroyed by Royal Mail since they were judged to be an infringement of copyright. Cauty took a different view of copyright and in any case he claimed to have invented copyright. Moreover he claimed to have invented the postage stamp in 2002 when he founded CNPD (Cautese Nationál Postal Disservice). Fifty-two first-day covers were produced, covering such topics as airplane and car disasters, Abbey Road, flying saucers (always popular), Che Guevara, a Bouguereau painting of the Virgin for Mother's Day, commemoration of the invention of the mobile phone, Pylon Day, Virgin and Vodafone.[149]

Mail Art had started in the 1960s and seems to have evolved in parallel with Fluxus, but it more narrowly stipulated that its creations should be posted. In theory, Mail Art suggested that anybody from anywhere could participate, regardless of their level of skill or expertise. For the American artist Walter Berman (1926–76) there was an added level of significance in that the transportation of the artefact through the postal system equates to a metaphysical act. The piece is transformed and carries the mark of this transformation through the acquisition of stamps, postmarks and the sense that it has passed through several hands 'absorbing energies'. The energies that were supposedly absorbed sound awfully like the 'vibes' that haunted the youth of the 1960s. Stuff was sent by mail and was validated as art by being posted. What was posted included collages, found objects and stamps created by artists. The stuff became art once it was despatched. It was seen as a way of circumventing the art establishment of dealers, critics, catalogues and museums.[150] Given the distrust felt by the Artistamp people towards the official postal service and museums, it is ironic that their first big publicity coup came through an exhibition of Mail Art and Artistamp in 1993 at Paris's Musée de la Poste.[151]

Mail Art participants used the postal service to confer an aura on the works they created. Mail Art and Artistamp people overlap, but Artistamp people are more narrowly dedicated to creating and exchanging their own stamps and stamp sheets. Theirs is a revolt against 'the philatelic world, ruled by precise laws and consolidated practices'. Official practices, postal regulations and the restrictive catalogues militate against the individual's right to produce 'these small objects of desire' (p.9). It has been suggested that one consequence of Fluxus and Artistamp has been a tendency for official postal issues to become more inventive and more artistic. This must be in the eye of the beholder.

Some artists took pleasure in slipping the stamps which they had created through the regular mail. In 1957 the French artist Yves Klein sent out invitation cards to an exhibition featuring canvases covered in a specific monochrome ultramarine blue which he claimed was uniquely his. The cards were blue and the stamps were too. He bribed the police to let them through the post. In quite another case three Italians specialised in creating bogus commemoratives and using them for the post, including such issues as 'The Mafia Olympic Games', 'The Festival of Stamp Forgers' and 'The World Streetwalkers Day'. When found out, they produced a further and final issue, 'Famous Stamp Forgers Arrested'.

In 1936 a series of Churchman's cigarette cards were issued which featured fifty (rather minor) celebrities. Number six in the series was W. Reginald Bray, 'The Human Letter':

> The owner of the largest collection of postal curios in the British Isles, Mr. Bray was the first man to post himself as a human letter. His collection was started as a hobby in 1898; he made a thorough study of the Post Office Guide and discovered that one of the smallest articles that can be sent by post is a bee, and the largest an elephant! Mr. Bray has posted many peculiar articles, including a shirt front and a collar with the addresses actually written upon them . . . Other things he has sent include a bowler hat, a turnip with the address and message carved on it, a pipe, cigarette flask, shoes, cycle pump, etc.

(Romford's leading rat catcher was celebrity number eleven in the cards.)

When Bray posted himself, the correct postage was clearly attached to his forehead. It may be tempting to see Mr Bray as a forerunner of the Mail Art movement, but Mr Bray seems to have been lacking in humour or any aesthetic sense. He seems rather to have been a dogged and very tiresome campaigner for citizens' rights. He had started out as a schoolboy stamp collector. But then in 1898 an ill fate placed a copy of the *Post Office Guide* in his hands. The *Guide* set out the generous limits to what it was and was not obliged to deliver so long as it had the right postage and was clearly addressed. So Bray set out to test the good will of the staff by posting a correctly addressed rabbit's skull, a piece of seaweed, a frying pan and so forth. On one occasion he posted a penny coin with a hole drilled through it, but forgot to add the stamp. So the Post Office charged him two pence for that.

Forgetting Bray's pioneering experiments (and from photographs he certainly was no hippy), the heyday of Fluxus and Mail Art seems to have been in the 1960s. These movements were of a piece with the 1960s novels of the American writer Thomas Pynchon (b.1937). He decided early in the 1960s to write three novels simultaneously. The first of these to be published, *V* (1963), was a complex, philosophically dense novel, in large part concerning a quest for a female spy, V, whose identity varied according to where in the novel she cropped up. The second novel, which came out in 1965, *The Crying of Lot 49*, is much shorter (45,000 words) but no less complex and at least as mysterious. The main storyline concerns what may be a paranoid philatelic fantasy set in what Pynchon characterised as 'a mad West Coast'. The protagonist, a young Californian woman, Oedipa Maas, is appointed co-executor of the estate of her former lover, the millionaire Pierce Inverarity, and this legacy includes a collection of rare stamps:

> Much of the revelation was to come through the stamp collection Pierce had left, his substitute often for her—thousands of little coloured windows into deep vistas of space and time: savannahs teeming with elands and gazelles, galleons sailing west into the void, Hitler heads, sunsets, cedars of Lebanon, allegorical faces that never were, he could spend hours peering into each one, ignoring her. She had never seen the fascination.[152]

Even so, not only are some of the stamps rare, but there is something rather strange about them, as she will discover when she takes the collection to be examined and evaluated by a philatelic expert, Genghis Cohen (a man who likes to have sex with the radio news on).

Oedipa is slowly led to believe that she has found evidence of a hidden alternative society whose members communicate with one another by letters which they post in special letterboxes, though to the uninitiated these letterboxes seem to be just waste bins. She goes to see a play from the Jacobean period, *The Courier's Tragedy* by Richard Wharfinger, and this imaginary drama is expertly summarised and parodied by Pynchon. In this play, Prince Niccolò, true heir to the Duchy of Faggio, has survived and disguised himself as a special courier of the monopolistic mail service run by the German state of Thurn and Taxis and made use of by the villainous Italian Duke Angelo. As was the convention in a seventeenth-century revenge tragedy, the plot that follows relies on conspiracy, incest, torture and bloodshed. In the fourth act Niccolò is despatched by Angelo with a letter to his hostile neighbour Gennaro, but Niccolò is killed before he can deliver the letter or claim his rightful inheritance. The letter that Niccolò was carrying is read out by Gennaro. It miraculously contains Angelo's confession of his evil deeds and includes some lines of (bad) poetry about the death of Niccolò, ending with the lines,

> He that we last as Thurn and Taxis knew
> Now recks no lord but stiletto's Thorn,
> And Tacit lies the gold once-knotted horn.
> No hallowed skein of stars can ward, I trow,
> Who's once been set his tryst with Trystero.

The fifth and final act is 'entirely an anti-climax'.[153]

The post horn (the same kind of instrument that De Quincey's coachman carried) was the symbol of the historic Thurn and Taxis postal service. Trystero, its secret and perhaps entirely fanciful rival, adopted the muted post horn as its symbol and now Oedipa starts to see the muted post horn scrawled as graffiti on a lavatory wall and then sundry unlikely places and, sometimes, this graffiti is accompanied by the letters W.A.S.T.E., which she is told is an acronym for 'We Await Tristero's Silent Empire'.

The 'languid sinister blooming of The Tristero' had begun. Then Oedipa is rung up by the philatelist, Genghis Cohen. He tells her that there are some disturbing irregularities in the stamps that she has left for him to examine and evaluate. She should come and see. When she arrives, he gives her a glass of dandelion wine and shows her a US stamp of 1940 commemorating the Pony Express. It looks normal, but when it is turned over, the W.A.S.T.E. symbol of the muted post horn can be seen to be its watermark. Quite a few of the stamps in Inverarity's collection are mocking forgeries, though, as Cohen explains, there are some collectors who specialise in forgeries and are prepared to pay a lot for them. The Tristero forgeries run back to 1893.[154]

Slowly Oedipa puts together what she learnt about Trystero (or Tristero). The small German state of Thurn and Taxis had run a monopolistic mail service from at least the sixteenth century onwards, but in 1577 Trystero was set up in Holland as a rival. Whereas Thurn and Taxis displayed a post horn as their emblem, their rival's emblem was the schematically depicted muted post horn. But, as the play lamented, Trystero had been defeated in Europe by the more orthodox (and historical) mail service. Yet Tristero survived and 'sometime before 1853 it had appeared in America and fought the Pony Express and Wells Fargo, either as outlaws in black, or disguised as Indians; and it survived into her own time in California, serving as a secretive, counter-cultural channel of communication for those of unorthodox sexual persuasion' (pp.81–2). Further researches by Genghis Cohen and by Bortz, the editor of *The Courier's Tragedy*, reveal that in the mid-nineteenth century the Tristero had indeed migrated to America. They were not looking for freedom from tyranny or anything like that. Instead the emphasis is on 'silence, impersonation, opposition masquerading as allegiance'. They will forge stamps that subtly impersonate and mock those of the US Mail. For example: 'In the 15c dark green from the Columbian Exposition Issue ("Columbus Announcing His Discovery"), the faces of the three courtiers, receiving the news at the right-hand side of the stamp, had been subtly altered to express uncontrollable fright' (pp.131–2).

Is this all simply a paranoid fantasy? The mood is that of a melancholy and erotic romance. There is a druggy feel to the supposed Tristero counterculture—and indeed to the whole novel—and drug taking and paranoia tend to run along together in fiction and reality. Or could the whole Tristero thing be a malevolent hoax against Oedipa which was posthumously launched by her embittered former lover, Inverarity? Or is it essentially some kind of confidential, weirdo dating agency? Or is Oedipa mad? Or is Tristero supposed to be a true feature of the madness of West Coast culture? Is Pierce's legacy a symbol of what America is?

Oedipa is confronted with a series of bizarre and puzzling subplots and mad cameo encounters. She learns about Inverarity's crooked scheme to use the ground-up bones of dead American Second World War soldiers as cigarette filters. She observes her husband, Mucho Maas, let himself be destroyed by an addiction to LSD. Dr Hilarius, her psychiatrist, turns out to have been a doctor at Buchenwald where he had worked at experimentally inducing insanity. She meets John Nefastis, a man obsessed with using Maxwell's demon to create a perpetual motion machine. She becomes the lover of Metzger, the former child actor and co-executor of Inverarity's will. She picks the brains of Mike Fallopian, a critical right-wing historian of the US postal system, and Professor Emory Bortz, the academic expert on *The Courier's Tragedy*.

The Tristero forgeries are to be sold at auction, listed as lot 49 (p.139). Will there be a Tristero bidder? But that is where the novel ends—with that final revelation withheld. The novel's ending is ostentatiously inconclusive. The muted post horn has warned us of silence and mystery. We can never know the truth about Inverarity's stamps. But, of course, to read Pynchon's remarkable novel primarily for its philatelic content is like reading *Lady Chatterley's Lover* for tips on game keeping. *The Crying of Lot 49* is not ultimately about stamps. It is a 1960s novel about the 1960s—so much sex, drugs and conspiracy theory, with almost nobody doing a proper job of work. All that and the oblique references to Beatlemania. The plot consists of it turning out to be no plot, since entropy has taken over the story. *The Crying of Lot 49* is a kind of detective novel in reverse in which, instead of things getting solved, they just get more and more mysterious.

Despite its fantastic nature, the Tristero movement that Pynchon has conjured up somewhat resembles both the real-life Mail Art movement and that of Artistamp. Moreover, the cocaine-addicted novelist and stamp collector Alex Trocchi would have been perfectly at home in Pynchon's book. A notoriously reclusive figure, Pynchon has not made himself available to be interviewed about *The Crying of Lot 49* or any of his other novels.

Pynchon's third novel, *Gravity's Rainbow*, was published in 1973. It is devoid of philatelic content and it has been followed by five more novels.

So now for Alexander Trocchi, who was born in Glasgow in 1925. After the war he spent time in France and the United States. In Paris he was swiftly recognised as a promising writer. He had also become a drug addict and he had published some short accounts of drug experiences and supported his habit by writing pornography. Having moved to New York in 1956, in 1960 he published *Cain's Book*, a lightly fictionalised autobiographical account of his time there as a user of cocaine and heroin, its miseries and difficulties and, inconsistently, an angry polemic in favour of the unrestricted use of hard drugs. Though the book was banned in Britain, it was widely available in the United States. He arrived back in Britain in 1963 and it is said that he was so happy to be in London that he resumed his childhood hobby of stamp collecting. As an adult he became an expert on stamp printing. He continued to deal in drugs as if it were his messianic mission and was widely regarded as a sinister and temperamental figure. But the journalist and critic A.A. Gill remembered him fondly: 'Alex, granite-faced, angry iconoclast, fearless nihilist, rager against the night, had managed to make heroin seem parochial, rather bourgeois. He'd done it for so long that it had become a pomade, a tonic, it never seemed to make any difference to his demeanour. I never saw him grouch or get scratchy.'[155] He died in 1984. An embittered and idle commentator of his times, he wrote nothing of significance after *Cain's Book*.

WHEREAS MAINSTREAM Freudian readings of collecting tend to lack a broad social context, the French sociologist Jean Baudrillard (1929–2007) maintained that the collector's need for a particular object was driven by a desire for social meaning. Baudrillard was most famous for his study of objects.[156] In this study he absorbed some elements of Freudian thinking. Thus the collector regresses to an anal phase, since the adult collector and the infant on his potty are both preoccupied with accumulation and retention. Yet Freud's propositions fell well short of Baudrillard's free-ranging thinking, a great deal of which seems to be inspired and dictated by his superbly aphoristic style.

He believed that consumption rather than production was the primary force in a capitalist society. The different ways things are consumed nowadays is something new in history. Collecting is one of the forms of consumption and, in Baudrillard's eyes, a degraded one.[157] In *Le Système des objets* (*The System of Objects*) Baudrillard presented what was sought after for a collection as 'objects of passion'. A collection was comprised of objects rather than things for use: 'For the child, collecting represents the most rudimentary way to exercise control over the outer world: by laying things out, grouping them, handling them. Swapping plays a role in introducing the child to social interactions. The active phase of collecting seems to occur between the ages of seven and twelve, during the period of latency prior to puberty.' Men in their forties may return to collecting. Peter Gay (see below) is an example of this phenomenon. The collection is a harem, a secluded area of intimacy. Collecting is an activity that abolishes time: 'It is clear that one does not collect Old Masters in the same spirit that one collects cigar bands.' (Yes, he must be right, but how is it so?) The typical collector nurses a passion not for possessing the objects themselves, but one that stems from his anxiety to achieve completeness. Such illusory wholeness might be thought to serve as a flight and a protection from other people—but it does not. In truth there is no pleasure in completeness, but only death.

By the way, the fanatical book collector John Baxter remembered an encounter with Josef von Sternberg:

> I once asked the film director Josef von Sternberg, Svengali of Marlene Dietrich and creator of *Shanghai Express* and *The Blue Angel*, whether he had a hobby.
>
> 'Yes,' grated the toneless voice, which still retained a whiff of the Vienna of Mahler and Freud. 'Chinese philately.' It wasn't what I expected to hear. 'Why that?'
>
> 'I wanted a subject I could not exhaust.'[158]

Baudrillard is only one of those theorists who have written about collecting and who have equated the completeness of a collection with death.

The Jewish historian and memoirist Peter Gay (1923–2015) grew up in Berlin. He fled from Nazi Germany in 1939 and subsequently had a successful career as an academic who specialised in European modern literature and intellectual life and became Professor of History at Yale. In a memoir devoted to his childhood in Germany, he recalled how he became absorbed in stamp collecting. This hobby not only served as an invisible barrier that cut him off from the Nazi-dominated city, but it bonded him with his father who also collected stamps. When he was eight or nine Peter's parents gave him a cheap beginner's stamp album. At first he specialised in British colonial islands and later he switched to German inflation issues. (The inflation ended in 1923.) His father followed him in stamp collecting, concentrating on German stamps and hard-to-get errors. He even bought Hitler stamps. For both it was 'an island of order'.[159]

Flash forward to 1961. While Peter Gay was teaching at Columbia University, he was drawn irresistibly to the New York department store of Gimbels, because it had a well-stocked philatelic counter: 'I started collecting stamps with much of the fervor I displayed for this pastime in my childhood. And it taught me something important about my six years in Nazi Germany: living there I had developed strategies for survival designed to keep me as sane as possible in the madhouse which the accident of birth and the perversity of history had thrown me.' (Jokes and sports also offered him other back-up strategies for survival (pp.92–3).)

The journalist and author Simon Garfield was born in 1960. Like Gay, he had collected stamps as a child and later returned to the activity as an adult, but things did not turn out so well for him. His memoir, *Error World: An Affair with Stamps*, is a sad yet very funny story, whose title draws on two sorts of error. First, like quite a few collectors, he specialised in errors: 'I don't collect ordinary stamps. I collect stamps with errors, with absent colours, with printing faults.' Specifically pre-decimal Queen Elizabeth II errors.[160] In the second sense, his return to stamp collecting as an adult brought him to the brink of emotional and financial ruin.

He was a child when he started collecting errors. Such stamps are mostly pretty rare and likely to be a bit expensive. (When one thinks about it, the high esteem in which errors are held by philatelists is a curious business. We do not normally make a cult of bad spelling, smudgy photographs or poor driving.) Garfield's first collection lasted from 1966 to 1973, though even as early as 1968 'it was a hobby that was falling away'. The competing demands of examinations and of attractive girls led to a waning of interest in stamps. Then it seems that it was a mid-life crisis that led him in his forties to return to stamp collecting and, when he did so, he started buying the stamps he could not have afforded as a child and soon he would be buying stamps that he could not afford as an adult. 'Little do wives know how much men spend on their hobbies.' A married man, his collecting was a secretive affair and his collection was a kind of mistress, but he had one of those as well. It all came out and, heavily in debt and divorced, he was driven to sell his collection of rare error stamps for £40,000. Perhaps he was like that kind of gambler for whom the attraction of betting is not the prospect of winning, but precisely the exciting risk of losing. His ex-wife had not been interested in used postage and the woman who succeeded her was not interested in stamps either. But Garfield adds, 'I am not sure that I could ever be attracted to any woman who was.'

And yet . . . 'As an alternative to religion and spirituality there are stamps, the quiet ordering of a life, the old-fashioned way of shutting out the world while bestowing it with meaning.' When one finishes *Error World* one knows that, for all the grief and loss, the small and silent world of stamps have not lost their charms for the author.

THE NOVELIST JULIAN BARNES published an essay on book collecting and completism, 'My Life as a Bibliophile', in which he suggested that owning objects that one had acquired functioned as a form of self-definition.[161] (Bachelard had also toyed with this notion.) Earlier, in a book largely consisting of reflections on death, he reflected upon his boyhood collecting of stamps. His grandmother, who had a sympathy for communist Cuba, passed on to him an assortment of Chinese stamps:

> These tended to celebrate industrial achievement—bridges, hydroelectric dams, lorries rolling off production lines—or else show various breeds of dove in flight . . . My brother did not compete for such offerings, because some years previously there had been a Stamp Collecting Schism in our home. He had decided to specialise in the British Empire. I, to assert my difference, announced that I would therefore specialize in a category which I named, with what seemed like logic to me, Rest of the World.[162]

This specialism 'later baffled fellow stamp collectors at school'.

As has already been noted, George Orwell regarded stamp collectors as a definite male type: 'stamp collectors are a strange, silent, fish-like breed, of all ages, but only of the male sex; women, apparently, fail to see the peculiar charm of gumming bits of coloured paper into albums'. So is there really a type? Can one smell a stamp collector? A category of man that would have to include Enrico Caruso, Franklin Delano Roosevelt, Edward Saïd, Prince Albert, Freddie Mercury, John Lennon, Yul Brynner, Gerald Ford, Jacques Cousteau, Simon Wiesenthal, Warren E. Buffett, Charlie Chaplin, Nicholas van Hoogstraten, George Bernard Shaw, Anatoly Karpov, Ronnie Wood, Nicolas Sarkozy, Alfred Kinsey and Chester Beatty? The description of such a type of man would have to be so broadly framed as to be worthless. It is true that there are fewer female philatelists whose names invite widespread recognition, but Ayn Rand has already been mentioned and Amelia Earhart,

Benazir Bhutto and Maria Sharapova are among the female stamp collectors of note.

The press commonly prefers to refer to the 'typical stamp collector' in jauntily disparaging tones. In an article by Stuart Millar in the *Guardian*, published to mark the opening of the 1996 Stampex exhibition in Islington, 'the most important bash in stamp collecting's crowded social calendar', he observes: 'Grey-haired men in herring-bone jackets poring intensely over stalls looking for treasure.' The royal collection was on display and in the case of a determined attempt at robbery by those attending the exhibition, the 'guards on duty would have struggled to withstand the determined onslaught from the doddery earnest-looking enthusiasts—all men apart from a few long-suffering wives—coming in to wonder at the first proofs of the Penny Black'. Millar's piece ends with a quotation from one of the collectors who was attending the fair. 'He was doing his best to convert non-believers. "I have never met a stamp collector who wasn't a very interesting person," he said with a straight face.' What comes over powerfully in all this is the journalist's need to distance himself from those with whom he mingles as he pumps them for good quotes. He is confident that the reader will share his patronising attitude. In what other context would such mockery of old men be so acceptable?

Walter Benjamin's delight in small things has been noted. Gaston Bachelard (1884–1962) was a scientific theorist and literary critic who was best known for his work on the epistemological breaks that he held to be evidence of the discontinuity of scientific progress. But it is *La Poétique de l'espace* (*The Poetics of Space*), one of his works on the poetics of daydreaming, or reverie, which concerns us here.[163] According to Bachelard, 'Daydream transports the dreamer outside the immediate world to a world that bears the mark of infinity.' One who daydreams dwells consciously or half-consciously on the look and feel of things in the immediate environment. And it is one, for daydreaming is a solitary activity. The daydreamer's house, which should be a home for his imagination, should have a cellar and an attic and in Bachelard's version of the 'House of Life', the cellar stands for the dark unconscious, while the attic for higher, more spiritual concerns. But *The Poetics of Space* also devotes a chapter to 'The Miniature', which is not restricted to the interior of the house. Here Bachelard begins by acknowledging that tiny things may take us back to fairy tales and childhood and the toys of childhood. 'But imagination deserves better than that,' according to Bachelard. 'In point of fact, imagination in miniature is natural imagination which appears at all ages in the daydreams of born dreamers' (p.149). The more the world is miniaturised in the imagination, the better it is possessed (p.150). 'The man with the magnifying glass—quite simply—bars the every-day world.' His use of a magnifying glass restores the child's-eye vision of the world:

> The botanist's magnifying glass is youth recaptured. It gives him back the enlarging gaze of a child . . . Thus the minuscule, a narrow gate, opens up an entire world. The details of a thing can be the sign of the new world, which, like all worlds, contains

> the attributes of greatness. Miniature is one of the refuges of greatness. (p.155)

Poetry is defended by Bachelard as a form of daydreaming. The argument is supported by citations of closely described tiny worlds by French poets who were often quite obscure figures. The somewhat confusing meditations on the homely visions of daydreaming poets left me wondering if Bachelard would have included the philatelist among those who use a magnifying glass to re-experience a child's-eye vision of the world.

> O! then I see, Queen Mab hath been with you . . .
> She is the fairies' midwife, and she comes
> In shape no bigger than an agate-stone
> On the forefinger of an alderman,
> Drawn with a team of little atomies
> Athwart men's noses as they lie sleep.
>
> (Mercutio, *Romeo and Juliet*, Act I, scene iv)

The miniature has the power to encompass much in little. So it draws its observer inwards and enthrals. As David Scott put it (perhaps overstressing the educational at the expense of the magical):

> The tiny format of the stamp works like a microcosm, offering a vision of the universe in which cultural and natural essences are concentrated. Sets of stamps offer the opportunity of creating

> a *musée imaginaire* of pictures, an anthology of poetic images. The stamp album becomes a kind of encyclopaedia, testifying to the splendour and diversity of the world; it is knowledge encapsulated in an idealised, almost imaginary form.[164]

John Ryle noted how the golden age of philately was coming to an end in the gaudy 1960s, the era of Tony Benn, when non-definitive stamps began to be designed to be primarily sold to collectors. Ryle's lament continued as follows:

> Indeed philately is not really a hobby anymore. Today's stamp collectors are more like curators. They are the custodians, not only of the childhood pleasures of people like myself, but of a global treasury of graphic design, cultural politics and nationalist mythology. At its best, the postage stamp is an extraordinary design achievement. A rare art of miniature, like a Moghul painting or an Elizabethan court portrait, one that should be more widely recognised, and one whose small compass should not obscure its wider significance, nor its intricate delights.[165]

Of course, miniaturisation does not always achieve the desired effect. Simon Garfield developed a strong antipathy to Israeli stamps: 'I found the Israeli stamps boring . . . they were seldom blessed with visits from the muse. Many stamps seemed to rely on things that were originally big—paintings, buildings—that were then made smaller and smaller the way people did when photocopiers first came out they weren't designed, they were miniaturised.'[166] The ugly miniaturised bill-poster look of Iranian stamps has already been mentioned.

With reference to Ryle's observation that stamp collectors are increasingly assuming the role of 'curators', the 1970s saw the beginning of the decline in ordinary stamp collecting on the part of enthusiastic amateurs and schoolboys, but by contrast, a boom in acquiring expensive selections of stamps as investment portfolios really got underway in the same decade. In the decades that immediately followed there was something of a slump, though not in the market for Chinese stamps. I had lunch once with a man who had a collection of rare Chinese stamps. He had never actually seen his collection. It had been bought for him by the firm of Stanley Gibbons as an investment portfolio. Perhaps it was being curated for a future generation.

What one collects should be useless. A person who hunts out different types of sick bags or Ming vases can only be deemed to be a collector if he or she has no practical use for sick bags or Chinese ceramics. In my case I acquire books. I have thousands of them, but I do not *collect* first editions, or books bound in vellum, or novels written by authors whose names begin with 'z'. Books are merely the tools of my trade. At one stage I did buy editions of the *Arabian Nights* and some related literature for serious work reasons. It was only when I started buying children's versions of *Arabian Nights* stories and colouring books, Japanese and Greek translations, worthlessly dim-witted academic analyses of the *Nights* and erotic renderings in *bandes dessinées* that I graduated and became a collector of the *Nights*.

I am an old man who is interested in stamps, exactly the sort of person pilloried by George Orwell and Stuart Millar, though I have never worn a herringbone jacket and will never gawp in awe at a proof copy of the Penny Black. I am more interested in the postage stamp as something that is good to think with.

When I started I could not know how this would end. A dream had set me off sleepwalking. I was not in control of what was coming. I could not know what would turn up. I had underestimated the intrinsic difficulty of the enterprise.

Over the decades I had become accustomed to writing about things which I knew a lot about, but with this book I found myself having to tackle subjects about which I knew more or less nothing and which sometimes I had never even heard of. And some of the material I felt that I had to discuss, for example the writings of Beckett, Braffort and Mandelstam, I did not fully understand, even after slowly reading what they had written and checking on the relevant secondary literature, but at other times I hoped to return to uncritical boyhood as I read the exciting adventures produced by Wheatley or Montsarrat. Either way I found myself trapped in what felt like a conceptual prison which was equipped with an unusually small and heterogeneous library. Over the years stamps have been served as such various signifiers and put to such different uses that one might just as well have written a book about the similarities and differences between a giraffe and a light bulb. But I chose to follow the dream.

And we are here as on a darkling plain
Swept with confused alarms of struggle and flight,
Where ignorant armies clash by night.[167]

Serendipity played a huge role in all this. Chance took precedence over diligence, erudition or logic. The collector in the fullest sense does not examine the listings in the catalogue before he finds the precise stamp he is looking for, regardless of the price, and then proceeds to Gibbons or some other similarly comprehensively stocked stamp shop where the stamp in question can be promptly located and sold to him. Instead the target stamp should preferably be discovered in a seedy little stamp shop presided over by a vendor who is half blind and quite ignorant. Alternatively the stamp might be passed on to the collector in an album whose owner, a cousin, has decided to give up stamp collecting. Or, best of all, a car boot sale. It is more or less the same with quotations. It would have given me little pleasure to find exactly what I wanted for my use in *The Penguin Dictionary of Philatelic Quotations*.

At this point I pause. I am about to fetch out my stamp albums. I have not as much as looked at them for over fifty years. So I shall be opening a time capsule. And the old man that I am will be communing with a youth that was. In a stark fashion it raises the question of individual identity, for, since I was a schoolboy, every atom, every idea and every sentiment of mine must have suffered a sea change. When I was young where did I imagine my stamp collection was going? Did I fantasise that with the passing of the decades my fourteen-kreuzer turquoise would have become incredibly rare? Would my collection fund my retirement? Should I anticipate myself as an old man ready to weep over his collection and the simple joys of boyhood? But then why should I? I am no longer a schoolboy and have no desire to return to that status. I think that what I fear most is that I shall feel nothing at all as I scan an accumulation of stuff gathered together by a stranger. For whatever reason, I lay on my bed full of a fear that I could not put a name to.

The time came when this possibly daft exercise in autoarchaeology could no longer be put off. I set to pulling the mostly bulky volumes from their place of storage. I had not guessed that there would be so many albums and so much dust on them. I kept making repeated trips to the bathroom to wash my hands. As I turned the pages my hope that memories of my boyhood would come flooding back were totally confounded, for, on the contrary, what I learned was how much I had not only forgotten but could also no longer retrieve. Where on the earth did that little album of Japanese pictorials come from? I think I was never keen on either Japanese stamps or pictorial issues. How did I acquire so many Latvian stamps? On what principle had some Iranian stamps been placed in one album and the rest in another? Those stamps covered in entirely indecipherable squiggles, where were they from? Why did I have no memory of visiting the Stockholm Stamp Museum? Above all, how had I acquired so many stamps, thousands of them? I was an enigma to myself.

Though the stamps spoke to me of the past, it was not my past, for overwhelmingly they bore witness to kingdoms, principalities and regimes that had perished before I had been born: the Kingdom of Bavaria, Hapsburg Austro-Hungary, Qajar Iran, the Ottoman Empire, the Kingdom of Hejaz and Nejd, the Chinese Treaty Ports, Hohenzollern Germany, Hyderabad. They carried images of men in regnal robes or uniforms (and the men were often bearded), ancient ruins, heraldry and paddle steamers. (There were no British stamps.) I had acquired a visual empire in a prolonged fit of absence of mind. As I gazed upon the albums on the floor, I was reminded of the treatment of old age and death in Iris Murdoch's *Bruno's Dream*, and a little later I decided that sorting out this vast accumulation of brightly coloured little bits of paper would occupy me very well in my declining years—perhaps in an old folks' home. As a boy I had prepared for my second childhood better than I knew.

ACKNOWLEDGEMENTS

The author wishes to thank Helen Irwin, Juri Gabriel, Phil Baker, John Ryle, Jane Dorner and Rory Williamson.

NOTES

1 Simon Garfield, *Error World: An Affair with Stamps* (London, 2008), p.71.
2 Thomas De Quincey, *The English Mail-Coach* (Oxford, 1985), pp.203–4.
3 Robert Morrison, *The English Opium Eater: A Biography of Thomas De Quincey* (London, 2009), p.363.
4 Maurice Keen, *Times Literary Supplement*, April 11, 1997.
5 Eric Hobsbawm, *Interesting Times: A Twentieth-Century Life* (London, 2002), p.9.
6 V.S. Naipaul, *A Bend in the River* (London, 2011), p.17.
7 Louis Aragon, *Paris Peasant*, tr. Simon Watson-Taylor (London, 1999), p.72.
8 David Benedictus, *The Stamp Collector* (London, 1994), p.67.
9 John Forrester, 'Freud and Collecting', in *The Cultures of Collecting*, ed. John Elsner and Roger Cardinal (London, 1994).
10 Werner Muensterberger, *Collecting: An Unruly Passion. Psychological Perspectives* (Princeton, NJ, 1994).
11 Mario Praz, *The House of Life*, tr. Angus Davidson (London, 1964).
12 Muensterberger, *Collecting*, pp.41–3.
13 Otto Fenichel, *The Psychoanalytic Theory of Neurosis* (London, 1946), p.283.
14 Ayn Rand, 'Why I Like Stamp Collecting', *Minkus Stamp Journal*, 6 (1971).
15 Christopher D. Johnson, *Memory, Metaphor, and Aby Warburg's Atlas of Images* (Ithaca, NY, 2012), p.67.
16 Kenneth Clark, *Another Part of the Wood: A Self-Portrait* (London, 1974), pp.189–90.
17 Roberto Calasso, 'The Art of Fiction', Interview, *The Paris Review*, 217 (2012), p.150.
18 Simon Schama, *Landscape and Memory* (London, 1995), p.213.
19 Ernst Gombrich, *Aby Warburg: An Intellectual Biography* (London, 1970), p.264.
20 Charlotte Schoell-Glass, '"Serious Issues": The Last Plates of Warburg's Picture Atlas *Mnemosyne*', in *Art History as Cultural History: Warburg's Projects*, ed. Richard Woodfield (Amsterdam, 2001), p.193.

21 Schama, *Landscape*, p.213.
22 Gombrich, *Aby Warburg*, pp.264–5.
23 David Scott, *European Stamp Design: A Semiotic Approach to Designing Messages* (London, 1995), pp.84–5.
24 Benedictus, *The Stamp Collector*, p.186.
25 Francis Spufford, *I May Be Some Time: Ice and the English Imagination* (London, 1996), pp.42–3.
26 Susan Sontag, Introduction to Walter Benjamin, *One-Way Street and Other Writings*, tr. Edmund F.N. Jephcott and Kingsley Shorter (London, 1979), p.17.
27 John Banville, 'By Lava Possessed', *New York Times*, August 9, 1992.
28 Susan Sontag, *The Volcano Lover* (London, 1992), pp.24–5.
29 Francis Spufford, ed., *The Chatto Book of Cabbages and Kings: Lists in Literature* (London, 1989), p.3.
30 Ciaran Carson, *The Star Factory* (London, 2019; first published 1997).
31 Italo Calvino, *A Collection of Sand: Essays*, tr. Martin McLaughlin (London, 2013), p.5.
32 Carson, *Star Factory*, pp.12–14.
33 Ciaran Carson, *Shamrock Tea* (London, 2001), p.19.
34 Ulrich Marzolph, 'The Sensitive Brothers and Their Clever Deductions', in *101 Middle Eastern Tales and Their Impact on Western Oral Tradition* (Detroit, MI, 2020).
35 Carson, *Shamrock Tea*, pp.241–2.
36 Sontag, *The Volcano Lover*, p.232.
37 Gershom Scholem, *Walter Benjamin: The Story of a Friendship*, tr. Harry Zohn (Philadelphia, PA, 1981), p.37.
38 Sontag, Introduction to Benjamin, *One-Way Street*, p.19.
39 Benjamin, tr. Jeffrey Mehlman, *London Review of Books*, September 8, 1994.
40 Benedictus, *Stamp Collector*, pp.119–20.
41 Walter Benjamin, 'Unpacking My Library: A Talk about Book Collecting', tr. Harry Zohn and reprinted in *Illuminations* (London, 1970), pp.61–9.
42 Benjamin, *One-Way Street*, p.92.
43 Walter Benjamin, 'Eduard Fuchs, Collector and Historian', in *One-Way Street*, pp.349–86 (p.361).
44 Dorothea Dietrich, *The Collages of Kurt Schwitters: Tradition and Innovation* (Cambridge, 1993), p.9.

45 Walter Benjamin, *The Arcades Project*, tr. Howard Eiland and Kevin McLaughlin (Cambridge, MA, 1999), p.430.

46 Naomi Schor, 'Collecting Paris', in *The Cultures of Collecting*, ed. Elsner and Cardinal.

47 Benjamin, 'First Sketches', in *The Arcades Project*, p.866.

48 Calvino, *Collection*, p.6.

49 Benjamin, *The Arcades Project*, pp.203–11.

50 Spufford, *Cabbages and Kings*, pp.15–16.

51 Susan Sontag, *Under the Sign of Saturn* (London, 1981), p.120.

52 George Melly, *Paris and the Surrealists* (London, 1991), p.80.

53 Aragon, *Paris Peasant*, p.15.

54 André Breton, *Nadja* (Paris, 1928). English translation, Richard Howard (London, 1960).

55 Peter Matussek, 'The Renaissance of the Theatre of Memory', *Janus*, 8 (2001), pp.1–9.

56 Calasso, 'The Art of Fiction', p.136.

57 Roberto Calasso, *The Ruin of Kasch*, tr. William Weaver and Stephen Sartarelli (London, 1995), p.341.

58 Reprinted in Calvino, *Collection*, pp.143–8.

59 Willy Eisenhart, *The World of Donald Evans* (New York, 1994).

60 Calvino, *Collection*, p.138.

61 Eisenhart, *The World*, p.16.

62 Calvino, *Collection*, p.142.

63 *The Paris Review*, 1975, quoted in Eisenhart, *The World*, p.9.

64 Eisenhart, *The World*, p.16.

65 Patrick Leigh Fermor, *A Time of Gifts. On Foot to Constantinople: From the Hook of Holland to the Middle Danube* (London, 1977), p.27.

66 Ciaran Carson, *Fishing for Amber: A Long Story* (London, 1999), p.4.

67 Eisenhart, *The World*, p.158.

68 Scott, *European Stamp Design*, p.37.

69 Scott, *European Stamp Design*, p.42.

70 Aragon, *Paris Peasant*, p.127.

71 Susan Stewart, *On Longing: Narratives of the Miniature, the Gigantic, the Souvenir, the Collection* (Durham, NC, 1993), pp.164–5.

72 Bruce Chatwin, 'The Album of Donald Evans', *The New York Review of Books*, May 14, 1981, pp.14–16; reprinted in *What Am I Doing Here* (London, 1989).

73 Susannah Clapp, *With Chatwin: Portrait of a Writer* (London, 1997), pp.91–3.
74 Spufford, *Cabbages and Kings*, p.4.
75 Benedictus, *The Stamp Collector*, p.97.
76 Bruno Schulz, *Sanatorium under the Sign of the Hourglass*, tr. Celina Wieniewska (London, 1979), pp.31–32.
77 Gershom Scholem, *Kabbalah* (Jerusalem, 1974), p.58.
78 Robert Irwin, 'Introduction' to Iris Murdoch, *Bruno's Dream* (London, 2000), pp.1–8.
79 Murdoch, *Bruno's Dream*, p.12.
80 Irwin, 'Introduction' to Murdoch, *Bruno's Dream*, p.7.
81 Louise Erdrich, *The Plague of Doves* (London, 2008).
82 Muensterberger, *Collecting*, p.9.
83 Philip Roth, *The Plot Against America* (London, 2004), pp.21–2.
84 Mervyn Peake, *Titus Alone*, p.77.
85 Benedictus, *The Stamp Collector*, p.115.
86 Phil Baker, *The Devil Is a Gentleman: The Life and Times of Dennis Wheatley* (Sawtry, 2011), p.515.
87 Graham Greene, *The Heart of the Matter* (London, 2004) pp.108–9.
88 Thomas De Quincey, 'Suspiria de profundis', in *Confessions of an English Opium Eater and Other Writings*, ed. Grevel Lindop (Oxford, 1985), pp.103–4.
89 Greene, *The Heart of the Matter*, p.5.
90 John Fowles, *The Journals*, 2 vols (London, 2009), vol.1, p.135.
91 John Fowles, *The Collector* (London, 1963), p.172.
92 John Fowles, *The Aristos* (London, 1968), p.ix.
93 Osip Mandelstam, 'The Egyptian Stamp', in *The Prose of Osip Mandelstam*, ed. and tr. Clarence Brown (Princeton, NJ, 1967). It was first published in Russia in 1928.
94 Daphne M. West, *Mandelstam: The Egyptian Stamp* (Birmingham, 1980).
95 Samuel Beckett, *Molloy*, trans. Patrick Bowles and Samuel Beckett (New York, 1955), pp.148–9; Phil Baker, 'The Stamp of the Father in *Molloy*', *Journal of Beckett Studies*, 5 (1995), pp.142–55.
96 Phil Baker, *Beckett and the Mythology of Psychoanalysis* (London, 1997).
97 Beckett, *Molloy*, pp.165–6.
98 Ciaran Carson, *Exchange Place* (Belfast, 2012), p.53.
99 Robert Louis Stevenson, *The Wrecker* (London, 1924), pp.321.
100 Ellery Queen, *The Chinese Orange Mystery* (New York, 2018), p.210. First edition 1934.

101 Queen, *Chinese Orange*, pp.16–19.
102 John Updike, *In the Beauty of the Lilies* (London, 1996), pp.110–12.
103 John Updike, 'Not Cancelled Yet' in *Selected Poems*, ed. Christopher Carduff (London, 2015).
104 Julio Cortázar, 'Poisons', in *Bestiary: Selected Stories*, tr. by various hands (London, 1998), pp.114–25.
105 Robert Irwin, 'Let's Look at the Records', *The New York Times*, October 15, 2000.
106 José Saramago, *All the Names*, tr. Margaret Jull Costa (London, 1999), p.13.
107 Hugh Lofting, *Doctor Dolittle's Post Office* (London, 1924), p.40.
108 David Langford, 'Pratchett, Terry', in *The Encyclopedia of Fantasy*, ed. John Clute and John Grant (London, 1997).
109 Terry Pratchett, *Going Postal* (London, 2004).
110 Bruce McCall, *Zany Afternoons* (London, 1983).
111 J.B. Morton, *The Best of Beachcomber*, ed. Michael Frayn (London, 1963), pp.79–80.
112 Umberto Eco, *The Mysterious Flame of Queen Loana*, tr. Geoffrey Brock (London, 2006), p.254.
113 An interview with Eco in the *Los Angeles Times*, June 13, 2005.
114 Orhan Pamuk, *The Museum of Innocence*, tr. Maureen Freely (London, 2010), pp.691–2, 697–8.
115 Orhan Pamuk, *The Innocence of Objects*, tr. Ekin Oklap (New York, 2012), p.46.
116 Orhan Pamuk, *The Innocence of Memories*, tr. Ekin Oklap (London, 2018), p.67.
117 Sontag quoted in Benjamin Moser, *Sontag: Her Life* (London, 2019), p.248.
118 Joseph Cornell, *Wanderlust*, exh. cat. (London, 2015), p.174.
119 J.B. Priestley, *Angel Pavement* (London, 1930), p.70.
120 Robert Opie, 'Unless you do these crazy things . . . ', in *The Cultures of Collecting*, ed. Elsner and Cardinal, p.29.
121 'The true paradises are the paradises that we have lost'; Marcel Proust, *Le Temps retrouvé* (*Time Regained*, 1926), in *Remembrance of Things Past*, tr. C.K. Scott-Moncrieff and S. Hudson.
122 Stewart, *On Longing*, p.23.
123 Bjørn Berge, *Nowherelands: An Atlas of Vanished Countries 1840–1975*, tr. Lucy Moffatt (London, 2017).
124 Alan Bennett, *The History Boys* (London, 2004), p.7.

125 E.S. Turner, 'Fernando Po and the Lost Lands', in *An ABC of Nostalgia: From Aspidistras to Zoot Suits* (London, 1984).

126 C. Montrésor, *Some Hobby Horses; or How to Collect Stamps, Coins, Seals, Crests and Scraps* (London, 1890), quoted in Stewart, *On Longing*, p.190.

127 Alastair Brotchie, *Alfred Jarry: A Pataphysical Life* (Cambridge, MA, 2011), pp.270–1.

128 Daniel Levin Becker, *Many Subtle Channels: In Praise of Potential Literature* (Cambridge, MA, 2012), pp.122–3.

129 David Bellos, *Georges Perec: A Life in Words* (London, 1999), pp.96–9, 397–8.

130 Paul Braffort, 'Yvert's Journey', tr. Ian Monk, in Georges Perec, *Winter Journeys* (London, 2013).

131 David Holden, *Farewell to Arabia* (London, 1966), p.73.

132 Holden, *Farewell*, pp.82–3. On Condé's military and philatelic career in the Middle East, see also Dana Adams Schmidt, *Yemen: The Unknown War* (London, 1968), pp.127–32.

133 Ronald Storrs, *Orientations* (London, 1943), p.189.

134 E.M. Dowson, *A Short Note on the Design and Issue of Postage Stamps Prepared by the Survey of Egypt for His Highness Hussein Emir & Sherif of Macca & King of the Hejaz* (El-Qahira, 1918).

135 L.N. Williams and M. Williams, *Cinderella Stamps* (London, 1970), p.1.

136 James Warren Felter, *Artistamps/Francobolli d'Artista* (Bertiolo, 2000), p.125.

137 Williams and Williams, *Cinderella Stamps*, p.81.

138 Felter, *Artistamps*, p.51.

139 Berge, *Nowherelands*, pp.220–2.

140 Felter, *Artistamps*, pp.140–9.

141 Erwin S. Strauss, *How to Start Your Own Country* (Port Townsend, WA, 1984).

142 A. Reynolds Morse, *The Quest for M.P. Shiel's Realm of Redonda* (Cleveland, OH, 1979); *The Kingdom of Redonda 1865–1990*, ed. Paul de Fortis (Wirral, 1990): Michael Hingston, *Try Not to Be Strange: The Curious History of the Kingdom of Redonda* (Windsor, ON, 2022).

143 Javier Marías, *All Souls*, tr. Margaret Jull Costa (London, 2012).

144 Javier Marías, *Dark Back of Time*, tr. Esther Allen (London, 2003), p.140.

145 Thomas De Quincey, 'Confessions of an English Opium Eater' in *Confessions of an English Opium Eater and Other Writings*, ed. Grevel Lindop (Oxford, 1985), p.48.

146 Varro E. Tyler, *Philatelic Forgers: Their Lives and Works* (London, 1976), pp.14–15.
147 *The Stamp Art and Postal History of Michael Thompson and Michael Hernandez de Luna* (Chicago, IL, 2000).
148 Luis R. González Manso, 'An Alien in My Mailbox', *Fortean Times*, December, 2022, pp.42–7.
149 James Cauty, *Stamps of Mass Destruction and Other Postal Disasters*, vol.1 (London, 1969), vol.2 (London, 2005).
150 On Mail Art and related movements, see Hervé Fischer *et al.*, *Art and Marginal Communication* (London, 2011); William Rowe, *Surreal Stickers and Unreal Stamps* (New York, 1983).
151 Felter, *Artistamps*, p.14.
152 Thomas Pynchon, *The Crying of Lot 49* (London, 1996), p.31.
153 Pynchon, *Crying*, pp.47–55.
154 Pynchon, *Crying*, pp.70–3.
155 A.A. Gill, *Pour Me: A Life* (London, 2015), p.12.
156 Jean Baudrillard, *Le Système des objets* (Paris, 1968). Translated into English as *The System of Objects*, tr. James Benedict (London, 1996).
157 In what follows, references are to the translation of Jean Baudrillard, 'A Marginal System: Collecting', included in *The Cultures of Collecting*, ed. Elsner and Cardinal.
158 John Baxter, *A Pound of Paper: Confessions of a Book Addict* (London, 2002), pp.12–13.
159 Peter Gay, *My German Question: Growing Up in Nazi Berlin* (New Haven, CT, 1998), pp.95–6.
160 Garfield, *Error World*, p.3.
161 Julian Barnes, 'My Life as a Bibliophile', *The Guardian*, June 29, 2012.
162 Julian Barnes, *Nothing to Be Frightened Of* (London, 2008), pp.2–3.
163 Gaston Bachelard, *The Poetics of Space*, tr. Maria Jolas (Boston, MA, 1994).
164 Scott, *European Stamp Design*, pp.13–14.
165 John Ryle, *The Guardian*, September, 1996.
166 Garfield, *Error World*, p.127.
167 Matthew Arnold, 'Dover Beach'.

AVAILABLE AND COMING SOON FROM PUSHKIN PRESS

Pushkin Press was founded in 1997, and publishes novels, essays, memoirs, children's books—everything from timeless classics to the urgent and contemporary.

Our books represent exciting, high-quality writing from around the world: we publish some of the twentieth century's most widely acclaimed, brilliant authors such as Stefan Zweig, Yasushi Inoue, Teffi, Antal Szerb, Gerard Reve and Elsa Morante, as well as compelling and award-winning contemporary writers, including Dorthe Nors, Edith Pearlman, Perumal Murugan, Ayelet Gundar-Goshen and Chigozie Obioma.

Pushkin Press publishes the world's best stories, to be read and read again. To discover more, visit www.pushkinpress.com.

THE PASSENGER
ULRICH ALEXANDER BOSCHWITZ

TENDER IS THE FLESH
NINETEEN CLAWS AND A BLACK BIRD
THE UNWORTHY
AGUSTINA BAZTERRICA

SOLENOID
MIRCEA CĂRTĂRESCU

THE WIZARD OF THE KREMLIN
GIULIANO DA EMPOLI

AT NIGHT ALL BLOOD IS BLACK
BEYOND THE DOOR OF NO RETURN
DAVID DIOP

WHEN WE CEASE TO UNDERSTAND THE WORLD

THE MANIAC

BENJAMÍN LABATUT

NO PLACE TO LAY ONE'S HEAD

FRANÇOISE FRENKEL

FORBIDDEN NOTEBOOK

ALBA DE CÉSPEDES

COLLECTED WORKS: A NOVEL

LYDIA SANDGREN

MY MEN

VICTORIA KIELLAND

AS RICH AS THE KING

ABIGAIL ASSOR

LAND OF SNOW AND ASHES

PETRA RAUTIAINEN

LUCKY BREAKS

YEVGENIA BELORUSETS

THE WOLF HUNT

AYELET GUNDAR-GOSHEN

MISS ICELAND

AUDUR AVA ÓLAFSDÓTTIR

MIRROR, SHOULDER, SIGNAL

DORTHE NORS

THE WONDERS

ELENA MEDEL

GROWN UPS

MARIE AUBERT